W9-BQS-453

Differentiating Instruction With Menus

Language Arts

Laurie E. Westphal

PRUFROCK PRESS INC.
WACO, TEXAS

Prufrock Press Inc.
P.O. Box 8813
Waco, TX 76714-8813
Phone: (800) 998-2208
Fax: (800) 240-0333
http://www.prufrock.com

For Stan, whose favorite subject was English.
Thanks for always having my back and "holding
my hand" when support is needed.

CONTENTS

Part 1
All About Choice
and Menus

CHAPTER 1

Choice

"**O**h my gosh! THAAAAANK YOU!" exclaimed one of my students as he fell to his knees dramatically in the middle of my classroom. I had just handed out a List Menu on the periodic table and told my class they would be able to choose how they wanted to learn the material.

Why Is Choice Important to Middle School Students?

> " . . . Almost every kid in middle school wants freedom of his or her choice of what they want to work on. They just do."
>
> *—Eighth-grade math student*

First, we have to consider who (or what) our middle school students personify. During these years, adolescents struggle to determine who they are and how they fit into the world around them. They constantly try new ideas (the hydrogen peroxide in the hair sounded like a good idea at the time), new experiences (if you sit on the second-floor roof of your home one more time, I will tell your parents!), and constant flux of personalities (preppy one day, dark nails and lipstick the next) in order to obtain "zen" and find themselves. During this process, which can take from a few months to a few years depending on the child, academics are not always at the forefront of his mind unless the student has chosen that as part of his identity. Knowing this, instruction and higher level products have to engage the individuals these students are trying to become.

> ## "I like choice because I get to make decisions on my own. For myself!"
> —*Seventh-grade science student*

Ask adults whether they would prefer to choose what to do or be told what to do, and of course, they are going to say they would prefer to have a choice. Students have the same feelings, especially middle school students. Academics usually have been pushed back in priority as they seek to find themselves, so implementing choice as a way to engage these students has many explicit benefits once it has been developed as the center of high-level thinking.

> ## "I like being able to choose, because I can pick what I am good at and avoid my weaknesses."
> —*Eighth-grade language arts student*

One benefit of choice is its ability to meet the needs of so many different students and their learning styles. The Dunedin College of Education (Keen, 2001) conducted a research study on the preferred learning styles of 250 gifted students. Students were asked to rank different learning options. Of the 13 different options described to the students, only one option did not receive at least one negative response, and that was the option of having a choice. Although all students have different learning styles and preferences, choice is the one option that can meet everyone's needs. Unlike elementary students, middle school students have been engaged in the learning process long enough that they usually can recognize their own strengths and weaknesses, as well their learning styles. By allowing choice, students are able to choose what best fits their learning styles and educational needs.

> **". . . I am different in the way I do stuff. I like to build stuff with my hands more than other things."**
> *—Sixth-grade student*

Another benefit of choice is a greater sense of independence for the students. What a powerful feeling! Students will be designing and creating a product based on what they envision, rather than what their teacher envisions. When students would enter my middle school classroom, they often had been trained by previous teachers to produce exactly what the teacher wanted, not what the students thought would be best. Teaching my students that what they envision could be correct (and wonderful) was a struggle. "Is this what you want? or "Is this right?" were popular questions as we started the school year. Allowing students to have choices in the products they create to show their learning helps create independence at an early age.

> **"It [choice] puts me in a good mood to participate!"**
> *—Seventh-grade student*

Strengthened student focus on the required content is a third benefit. Middle school students already have begun to transition from an academic focus to more of a social one. Choice is a way to help bring their focus back to the academic aspect of school. When students have choices in the activities they wish to complete, they are more focused on the learning that leads to their choice product. Students become excited when they learn information that can help them develop a product they would like to create. Students will pay close attention to instruction and have an immediate application for the knowledge being presented in class. Also, if students are focused, they are less likely to be off task during instruction.

Many a great educator has referred to the idea that the best learning takes place when the students have a desire to learn. Some middle school students still have a desire to learn anything that is new to them, but many others do not want to learn anything unless it is of interest to them. By incorporating different activities from which to choose, students stretch beyond what they already know, and teachers create a void that needs to be filled. This void leads to a desire to learn.

How Can Teachers Provide Choices?

"The GT students seem to get more involved in assignments when they have choice. They have so many creative ideas and the menus give them the opportunity to use them."

—Social studies teacher

When people go to a restaurant, the common goal is to find something on the menu to satisfy their hunger. Students come into our classrooms having a hunger as well—a hunger for learning. Choice menus are a way of allowing our students to choose how they would like to satisfy that hunger. At the very least, a menu is a list of choices that students use to choose an activity (or activities) they would like to complete to show what they have learned. At best, it is a complex system in which students earn points by making choices from different areas of study. All menus also should incorporate a free-choice option for those "picky eaters" who would like to place a special order to satisfy their learning hunger.

Tic-Tac-Toe Menu

"They [Tic-Tac-Toe Menus] can be a real pain. A lot of times I only liked two of the choices and had to do the last one. Usually I got stuck with a play or presentation."

—Sixth-grade math student (asked to step out of her comfort zone based on the tic-tac-toe design)

Description

The Tic-Tac-Toe menu (see Figure 1.1) is a basic menu with a total of eight predetermined choices and one free choice for students. All choices are created at the same level of Bloom's Revised taxonomy (Anderson et al., 2001). All carry the same weight for grading and have similar expectations for completion time and effort.

Benefits

Flexibility. This menu can cover one topic in depth, or three different objectives. When this menu covers just one objective, students have the option of completing three products in a tic-tac-toe pattern, or simply picking three from the menu. When it covers three objectives, students will need to complete a tic-tac-toe pattern (one in each column or row) to be sure they have completed one activity from each objective.

Friendly Design. Students quickly understand how to use this menu.

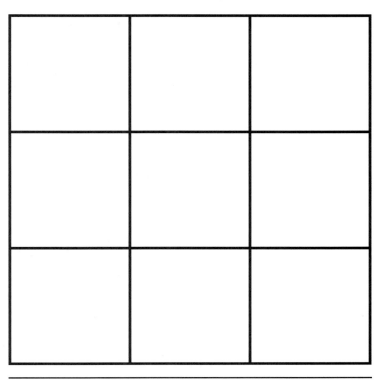

Figure 1.1. Tic-tac-toe menu.

Weighting. All products are equally weighted, so recording grades and maintaining paperwork is easily accomplished with this menu.

Limitations

Few Topics. These menus only cover one or three topics.

Short Time Period. They are intended for shorter periods of time, between 1–3 weeks.

Student Compromise. Although this menu does allow choice, a student will sometimes have to compromise and complete an activity he or she would not have chosen because it completes his or her tic-tac-toe. (This is not always bad, though!)

Time Considerations

These menus usually are intended for shorter amounts of completion time—at the most, they should take 3 weeks. If it focuses on one topic in-depth, the menu could be completed in one week.

List Menu

> "I like that you can add up the points to be over 100, so even if you make some small mistakes, your grade could still be a 100."
>
> *–Seventh-grade student*

Description

The List Menu (see Figure 1.2), or Challenge List, is a more complex menu than the Tic-Tac-Toe Menu, with a total of at least 10 predetermined choices, each with its own point value, and at least one free choice for students. Choices are simply listed with assigned points based on the levels of Bloom's Revised taxonomy. The choices carry different weights and have different expectations for completion time and effort. A point criterion is set forth that equals 100%, and students choose how they wish to attain that point goal.

Benefits

Responsibility. Students have complete control over their grades. They really like the idea that they can guarantee their grade if they complete their required work. If they lose points on one of the chosen assignments, they can complete another to be sure they have met their goal points.

Concept Reinforcement. This menu also allows for an in-depth study of material; however, with the different levels of Bloom's Revised taxonomy being represented, students who are still learning the concepts can choose

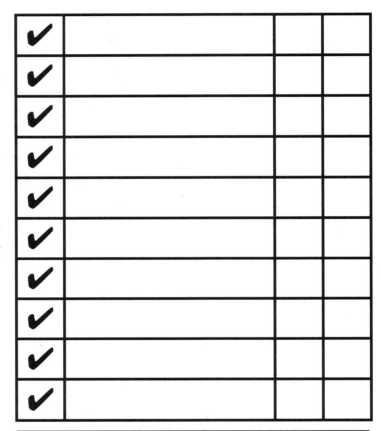

Figure 1.2. List menu.

some of the lower level point value projects to reinforce the basics before jumping into the higher level activities.

Limitations

Few Topics. This menu is best used for one topic in depth, although it can be used for up to three different topics.

Cannot Guarantee Objectives. If it is used for three topics, it is possible for a student to not have to complete an activity for each objective, depending on the choices he or she makes.

Preparation. Teachers need to have all materials ready at the beginning of the unit for students to be able to choose any of the activities on the list, which requires advanced planning.

Time Considerations

These menus usually are intended for shorter amounts of completion time—at the most, 2 weeks.

2–5–8 or 20-50-80 Menu

> "My least favorite menu is 2-5-8. You can't just do the easy ones. If you pick a 2, then you gotta do an 8, or you have to do 2 5s. I don't think you should do any more of these. No matter what you had to do one of hard ones."
>
> —*Seventh-grade student*

Description

A 2-5-8 Menu (see Figure 1.3), or 20-50-80 Menu, has two variations: one in which the activities are worth 2, 5, or 8 points, and one in which the activities are worth 20, 50, or 80. The 20, 50, and 80 version often is easier to grade with a rubric based on 5s (like the one included in this book). Both are variations on a List Menu, with a total of at least eight predetermined choices: at least two choices with a point value

Figure 1.3. 2-5-8 menu.

of 2 (20), at least four choices with a point value of 5 (50), and at least two choices with a point value of 8 (80). Choices are assigned these points based on the levels of Bloom's Revised taxonomy. Choices with a point value of two represent the *remember* and *understand* levels, choices with a point value of five represent the *apply* and *analyze* levels, and choices with a point value of eight represent the *evaluate* and *create* levels. All levels of choices carry different weights and have different expectations for completion time and effort. Students are expected to earn 10 (100) points for a 100%. Students choose what combination they would like to use to attain that point goal.

Benefits

Responsibility. With this menu, students still have complete control over their grades.

Guaranteed Activity. This menu's design also is set up in such a way that students must complete at least one activity at a higher level of Bloom's Revised taxonomy in order to reach their point goal.

Limitations

One Topic. Although it can be used for more than one topic, this menu works best with in-depth study of one topic.

No Free Choice. By nature, it also does not allow students to propose their own free choice, because point values need to be assigned based on Bloom's Revised taxonomy.

Higher Level Thinking. Students will complete only one activity at a higher level of thinking.

Time Considerations

These menus are usually intended for a shorter amount of completion time—at the most, one week.

Baseball Menu

> "There were so many choices and most of them were fun activities!"
>
> —Sixth-grade student

Description

This menu (see Figure 1.4) is a baseball-based variation on the List Menu, with a total of at least 20 predetermined choices: Choices are given values as singles, doubles, triples, or home runs based on Bloom's Revised taxonomy. Singles represent the *remember* and *understand* levels; doubles, the *apply* and *analyze* levels; triples, the *evaluate* level; and home runs, the *create* level. All levels of choices carry different weights and have different expectations for completion time and effort. Students are expected to earn a certain number of runs (around all four bases) for a 100%. Students choose what combination they would like to use to attain that number of runs.

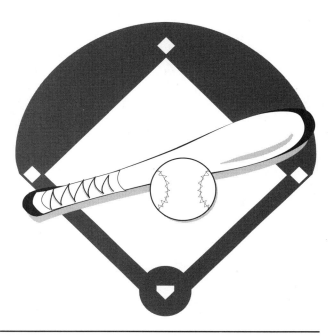

Figure 1.4. Baseball menu.

Benefits

Responsibility. With this menu, students still have complete control over their own grades.

Flexibility. This menu allows for many choices at each level. Students should have no trouble finding something that catches their interest.

Theme. This menu has a fun theme that students enjoy and can be used throughout the classroom. A bulletin board can be set up with a baseball diamond, with each student having his or her own player who can move through the bases. Not only can students keep track of their own RBIs, but they can have a visual reminder of what they have completed as well.

Limitations

One Topic. This menu is best used for one topic with many objectives for in-depth study.

Preparation. With so many choices available to students, teachers should have all materials ready at the beginning of the unit for students to be able to choose any of the activities on the list. This sometimes is a consideration for space in the classroom.

One Free Choice. This menu also only has one opportunity for free choice for students, in the home run section.

Time Considerations

These menus usually are intended for a longer amount of completion time, depending on the number of runs required for a 100%. At most, these are intended for 4 or 5 weeks.

Game Show Menu

"This menu really challenged my students. If one of my students saw another student choosing a more difficult option, they wanted to choose one, too. I had very few students choose to the basic options on this menu. It was wonderful!"

—*Sixth-grade science teacher*

Description

The Game Show Menu (see Figure 1.5) is the most complex menu. It covers multiple topics or objectives with at least three predetermined choices and a free student choice for each objective. Choices are assigned points based on the levels of Bloom's Revised taxonomy. All choices carry different weights and have different expectations for completion time and effort. A point criterion is set forth that equals 100%. Students must complete at least one activity from each objective in order to reach their goal.

Benefits

Free Choices. This menu allows many choices for students, but if they do not want to complete the offered activities, they can propose their own activity for each objective.

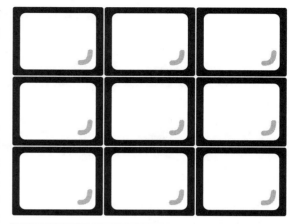

Figure 1.5. Game show menu.

Responsibility. This menu allows students to guarantee their own grades.

Different Learning Levels. It has the flexibility to allow for individualized contracts for different learning levels within the classroom. Each student can create a contract for a certain number of points for his or her 100%.

Objectives Guaranteed. The teacher is guaranteed that the students complete an activity from each objective covered, even if it is at a lower level.

Limitations

Confirm Expectations. The only real limitation here is that students (and parents) must understand the guidelines for completing the menu.

Time Considerations

These menus usually are intended for a longer amount of completion time. Although they can be used as a yearlong menu (each column could be a grading period), they usually are intended for 4–6 weeks.

Free Choice

"I don't know if I really liked it at first. It's a lot easier to just do the basic stuff and get it over with but when Mrs. [teacher] told us she wanted us to submit at least one free choice, I really got into it! I mean, I could do something I wanted to do? How often do you get to do THAT in school?"

—Eighth-grade GT student

With most of the menus, the students are allowed to submit a free choice for their teacher's consideration. Figure 1.6 shows two sample proposal forms that have been used successfully in my classroom. With middle school students, this cuts down greatly on the whining that often accompanies any task given to students. A copy of these forms should be given to each student when the menu is first introduced. The form used is based on the type of menu being presented. For example, if you are using the Tic-Tac-Toe Menu, there is no need to submit a point proposal. A discussion should be held with the students so they understand the expectations of a free choice. I always have a few students who do not want to complete a task on the menu; they are welcome to create their own free choice and submit it for approval. The biggest complainers will not always go to the trouble to complete the form and have it approved, but it is their choice not to do so. The more free choice is used and encouraged, the more students will begin to request it. How the students show their knowledge will begin to shift from teacher-focused to student-designed activities. If students do not want to make a proposal using the proposal form after the teacher has discussed the entire menu and its activities, they can place the unused form in a designated place in the classroom. Others may want to use their form, and it often is surprising who wants to submit a proposal form after hearing about the opportunity!

Proposal forms must be submitted before students begin working on their free-choice products. The teacher then knows what the students are working on and the students know the expectations the teacher has for that product. Once approved, the forms easily can be stapled to the students' menu sheets. The students can refer to it as they develop their free-choice product, and when the grading takes place, the teacher can refer to the agreement for the graded features of the product.

Name: _____   Teacher's Approval: _____

Free-Choice Proposal Form for Point-Based Menu

Points Requested: _____   Points Approved: _____

<u>Proposal Outline</u>

1. What specific topic or idea will you learn about?

2. What criteria should be used to grade it? (Neatness, content, creativity, artistic value, etc.)

3. What will your product look like?

4. What materials will you need from the teacher to create this product?

Name: _____   Teacher's Approval: _____

Free-Choice Proposal Form

<u>Proposal Outline</u>

1. What specific topic or idea will you learn about?

2. What criteria should be used to grade it? (Neatness, content, creativity, artistic value, etc.)

3. What will your product look like?

4. What materials will you need from the teacher to create this product?

Figure 1.6. Sample proposal forms for free choice.

Each part of the proposal form is important and needs to be discussed with students.

- *Name/Teacher's Approval.* The student must submit this form to the teacher for approval. The teacher will carefully review all of the information, send it back to the student for correction, if needed, and then sign the top.

- *Points Requested.* Found only on the point-based menu proposal form, this usually is where negotiation needs to take place. Students usually will submit their first request for a very high number (even the 100% goal.) They equate the amount of time something will take with the amount of points it should earn. But, please note, the points are *always* based on the levels of Bloom's Revised taxonomy. For example, a PowerPoint presentation with a vocabulary word quiz would get minimal points, although it may have taken a long time to create. If the students have not been exposed to the levels of Bloom's Revised taxonomy, this can be difficult to explain. You always can refer to the popular "Bloom's Verbs" to help explain the difference between time requirements and higher level activities.

- *Points Approved.* Found only on the point-based menu proposal form, this is the final decision recorded by the teacher once the point haggling is finished.

- *Proposal Outline.* This is where the student will tell you everything about the product he or she intends to complete. These questions should be completed in such a way that you can really picture what the student is planning on completing. This also shows you that the student knows what he or she is planning on completing.

- *What specific topic or idea will you learn about?* Students need to be specific here. It is not acceptable to write *science* or *reading.* This is where they look at the objectives of the product and choose which objective their product demonstrates.

- *What criteria should be used to grade it?* Although there are rubrics for all of the products that the students might create, it is important for the students to explain what criteria are most important to evaluate the product. The student may indicate that the rubric being used for all of the predetermined products is fine; however, he or she also may want to add other criteria here.

- *What will your product look like?* It is important for this to be as detailed as possible. If a student cannot express what it will "look like," he or she has probably not given the free-choice plan enough thought.

- *What materials will you need from the teacher to create this product?* This is an important consideration. Sometimes students do not have the means to purchase items for their product. This can be negotiated as well, but if you ask what students may need, they often will develop even grander ideas for their free choice.

CHAPTER 2

How to Use Menus in the Classroom

There are different ways to use instructional menus in the classroom. In order to decide how to implement each menu, the following should be considered: How much prior knowledge of the topic being taught do the students have before the unit or lesson begins, and how much information is readily available for students to obtain on their own? After considering these two questions, there are three customary ways to use menus in the classroom.

Enrichment and Supplemental Activities

Using the menus for enrichment and supplementary activities is the most common way to implement this tool. Usually, the teacher will introduce the menu and the activities at the beginning of the unit. In this case, the students usually do not have a lot of background knowledge and the information about the topic may not be readily available to all students. The teacher then will progress through the content at the normal rate using his or her curricular materials, periodically allowing class and homework time throughout the unit for students to work on their menu choices to supplement a deeper understanding of the lessons being taught. This method is very effective, as it builds in an immediate use for the content the teacher is covering. For example, at the beginning of a unit on mixtures, the teacher many introduce the menu with the explanation that students may not have all of the knowledge to complete all of their choices yet. During the unit, however, more content will be provided and the students will be prepared to work on new choices. If students want to work ahead, they certainly can find the information on their own, but that is not required. Gifted students often see this as a challenge and will begin to investigate concepts mentioned in the menu before the teacher introduces them. This helps build an immense pool of background knowledge before the topic is even discussed in the classroom. As teachers, we fight the battle of having students read ahead or "come to class prepared to discuss." By introducing a menu at the beginning of a unit and allowing students to complete products as instruction progresses, the students naturally investigate the information and come to class prepared without it being a completely separate requirement.

Standard Activities

Another option for using menus in the classroom is to replace certain curricular activities the teacher uses to teach the specified content. In this case, the students may have some limited background knowledge about the content, and information is readily available for them in their classroom resources. The teacher would pick and choose which aspects of the content must be directly taught to the students and which could be appropriately learned and reinforced through product menus. The unit then is designed using both formal instructional lessons and specific menu days where the students will use the menu to reinforce the prior knowledge they already have learned. In order for this option to be effective, the teacher must feel very comfortable with the students' prior knowledge level. Another variation on this method is using the menus to drive center or station activities. Centers have many different functions in the classroom—most importantly reinforcing the instruction that has taken place. Rather than having a set rotation for centers, the teacher could use the menu activities as enrichment or supplementary activities during center time for those students who need more than just reinforcement; centers could be set up with the materials students would need to complete various products.

Mini-Lessons

The third option for menu use is the use of mini-lessons, with the menus driving the accompanying classroom activities. This method is best used when the majority of the students have a lot of prior knowledge about the topic. The teacher would design short 10–15-minute mini-lessons, where students would quickly review or introduce basic concepts that already are familiar to them. The students then are turned loose to choose an activity on the menu to show they understand the concept. The Game Show Menu usually works very well with this method of instruction, as the topics across the top usually lend themselves very well to the mini-lessons. It is important that the students have prior knowledge on the content because the lesson cycle is cut very short in this use of menus. Using menus in this way does not allow the guided practice step of the lesson, as it is assumed the students already understand the information. The teacher simply is reviewing the information and then moving right to the higher levels of Bloom's Revised taxonomy by asking students to create a product. By using the menus in this way, the teacher avoids the "I already know this" glossy looks from his or her students. Another important consideration is the independence level of the students. In order for this use of menus to be effective, students will need to be able to work independently for up to 30 minutes after the mini-lesson. Usually because interest is high in the product they have chosen, this is not a critical issue, but still one worth mentioning as teachers consider how they would like to use various menus in their classroom. Menus can be used in many different ways; all are based on the knowledge and capabilities of the students working on them!

CHAPTER 3

Guidelines
for Products

". . . I got to do a play! In math!!"

—Seventh-grade student

This chapter outlines the different types of products included in the featured menus, as well as the guidelines and expectations for each. It is very important that students know the expectations of a completed product when they choose to work on it. By discussing these expectations *before* students begin and having the information readily available for students, you will limit frustration on everyone's part.

$1 Contract

Consideration should be given to the cost of creating the products in any menu. The resources available to students vary within a classroom, and students should not be graded on the amount of materials they can purchase to make a product look better. These menus are designed to equalize the resources students have available. The materials for most products are available for less than a dollar and often can be found in a teacher's classroom as part of the classroom supplies. If a product requires

```
┌─────────────────────────────────────────────────────────────────┐
│                        $1 Contract                                │
│                                                                   │
│  I did not spend more than $1.00 on my _____.  │
│                                                                   │
│                                                                   │
│  _____      _____            │
│           Student Signature                  Date                 │
│                                                                   │
│  My child, _____, did not spend more than $1.00 on the product │
│  he or she created.                                               │
│                                                                   │
│                                                                   │
│  _____      _____            │
│           Parent Signature                   Date                 │
│                                                                   │
└─────────────────────────────────────────────────────────────────┘
```

Figure 3.1. $1 contract.

materials from the student, there is a $1 contract as part of the product criteria. This is a very important piece in the explanation of the product. First of all, by limiting the amount of money a child can spend, it creates an equal amount of resources for all students. Second, it actually encourages a more creative product. When students are limited by the amount of materials they can readily purchase, they often have to use materials from home in new and unique ways. Figure 3.1 is a sample $1 contract that has been used many times in my classroom with various products.

The Products

Table 3.1 contains a list of the products used in this book. These products were chosen for their flexibility in meeting learning styles, as well as for being products many teachers already encourage in their classroom. They have been arranged by learning style—visual, kinesthetic, or auditory—and each menu has been designed to include products from all of the learning styles. Of course, some of the products may be listed in more than one area depending on how they are presented or implemented. The specific expectations for all of the products are presented in an easy-to-read card format that can be reproduced for students (see Figure 3.2).

The format is convenient for students to have in front of them when they work on their products. These cards also can be laminated and posted

Table 3.1
Products

Visual	Kinesthetic	Auditory
Acrostic	Board Game	Children's Book
Advertisement	Bulletin Board Display	Commercial
Book Cover	Class Game	Game Show
Brochure/Pamphlet	Commercial	Interview
Bulletin Board Display	Concentration Cards	News Report
Cartoon/Comic Strip	Cross-Cut Model	Play/Skit
Children's Book	Diorama	PowerPoint—Speaker
Collage	Flipbook	Presentation of Created
Cross-Cut Diagram	Folded Quiz Book	Product
Crossword Puzzle	Game Show	Puppet
Diary/Journal	Mobile	Song/Rap
Drawing	Model	Speech
Essay	Mural	Student-Taught Lesson
Folded Quiz Book	Museum Exhibit	Video
Greeting Card	Play/Skit	You Be the Person
Instruction Card	Product Cube	Presentation
Letter	Puppet	
Map	Quiz Board	
Mind Map	Science Experiment	
Newspaper Article	Student-Taught Lesson	
Paragraph	Survey	
Pie Graph	Three-Dimensional	
Poster	Timeline	
PowerPoint—Stand Alone	Trophy	
Questionnaire	Video	
Quiz		
Quiz Board		
Recipe/Recipe Card		
Scrapbook		
Story		
Survey		
Three Facts and a Fib		
Trading Cards		
Venn Diagram		
WebQuest		
Windowpane		
Worksheet		

on a bulletin board for easy access during classroom work. Some teachers prefer to only give a few product guidelines at a time, while others will provide all of the pages so students feel comfortable venturing out in their free choices. Students enjoy looking at all of the different products and it can stimulate ideas as they peruse the guidelines.

One of the most commonly used products in a language arts classroom is the story map. The story map is a quick and effective way for a student to dissect a story and show that he or she can identify and analyze the important parts of the story. Story maps are an option for most of the novel menus provided in this book. An example is provided (see Figure 3.3); however, teachers who have a favorite format that students are accustomed to should feel free to use their own.

Another product commonly referred to is a play or skit. Teachers may tend to shy away from this type of product because a 2-minute play can become a 20-minute ordeal between the paper shuffling and restarts. One of the easiest ways to handle this situation is to have students make appointments to come before or after school or during a teacher's conference period to record their plays as videos. The recording can be submitted for grading and the video or DVD can be shown at the teacher's leisure; days when there are sudden schedule changes are great for showing these productions.

Acrostic	Advertisement	Board Game
• At least 8.5" by 11" • Neatly written or typed • Target word will be written down the left side of the paper • Each descriptive phrase chosen must begin with one of the letters from the target word • Each descriptive phrase chosen must be related to the target word	• At least 8.5" by 11" • A slogan should be included • Color picture of item or service • Include price, if appropriate • Can be developed on the computer	• At least 4 thematic game pieces • At least 25 colored/thematic squares • At least 20 question/activity cards • Include a thematic title on the board • Include a complete set of rules for playing the game • At least the size of an open file folder
Book Cover	**Brochure/Pamphlet**	**Bulletin Board Display**
• Front cover—title, author, image • Cover inside flap—paragraph summary of the book • Back inside flap—brief biography of author with at least five details • Back cover—editorial comments about the book • Spine—title and author	• At least 8.5" by 11" • Must be in three-fold format; front fold has the title and picture • Must have both pictures and written text • Information should be in paragraph form with at least five facts included • Bibliography should be provided as needed • Can be created on computer • Any pictures from Internet must have proper credit	• Must fit within assigned space on bulletin board or wall • Must include at least 10 details • Must have a title • Must have at least five different elements (posters, papers, questions, etc.) • Must have at least one interactive element that engages the reader • $1 contract signed
Cartoon/Comic Strip	**Children's Book**	**Class Game**
• At least 8.5" by 11" • At least six cells • Must have meaningful dialogue • Must include color	• Must have a cover with book's title and student's name as author • Must have at least 10 pages • Each page should have an illustration to accompany the story • Should be neatly written or typed • Can be developed on the computer	• Game will allow everyone in the classroom to participate • Must have only a few, easy-to-understand rules • Should be inventive or a new variation on a current game • Must have multiple question opportunities • Must provide answer key before the game is played • The game must be approved by the teacher before being scheduled for play
Collage	**Commercial**	**Concentration Cards**
• At least 8.5" by 11" • Pictures must be cut neatly from magazines or newspapers (no clip art) • Label items as required in task	• Must be 2–4 minutes in length • Script must be turned in before commercial is presented • Can be presented live to an audience or recorded on a VHS tape or DVD • Should have props or some form of costume(s) • Can include more than one person	• At least 20 index cards (10 matching sets) must be made • Both pictures and words can be used • Information should be placed on just one side of each card • Include an answer key that shows the matches • All cards must be submitted in a carrying bag

Figure 3.2. Product guidelines.

Cross-Cut Model/Diagram	Crossword Puzzle	Diary/Journal
• Must include a scale to show the relationship between the product and the actual item • Must include details about each layer • If creating a model, also must meet the criteria of a model • If creating a diagram, also must meet the criteria of a poster	• At least 20 significant words or phrases should be included • Develop appropriate clues • Include puzzle and answer key • Can be created on the computer	• Neatly written or typed • Should include the appropriate number of entries • Should include a date if appropriate • Should be written in first person
Diorama	**Drawing**	**Essay**
• At least 4" by 5" by 8" • Must be self-standing • All interior space must be covered with relevant pictures and information • Name written on the back in permanent ink • Informational/title card attached to diorama • $1 contract signed	• Must be at least 8.5" by 11" • Must show what is requested in the task statement • Must include color • Must be neatly drawn by hand • Must have title • Name should be written on the back	• Must be neatly written or typed • Must cover the specific topic in detail • Must be at least three paragraphs • Must include resources or bibliography if appropriate.
Flipbook	**Folded Quiz Book**	**Game Show**
• At least 8.5" by 11" folded in half • All information or opinions are supported by facts • Created with the correct number of flaps cut into the top • Color is optional • Name must be written on the back	• At least 8.5" by 11" folded in half • At least 10 questions • Created with the correct number of flaps cut into the top • Questions written or typed neatly on upper flaps • Answers written or typed neatly inside each flap • Color is optional • Name written on the back	• Needs an emcee or host. • Must have at least two contestants • There must be at least one regular round and a bonus round • Questions will be content specific • Props can be used, but are not mandatory
Greeting Card	**Instruction Card**	**Interview**
• Front—colored pictures, words optional • Front inside—personal note related to topic • Back inside—greeting or saying; must meet product criteria • Back outside—logo, publisher, and price for card	• No larger than 5" by 8" • Created on heavy paper or card • Neatly written or typed • Uses color drawings • Provides instructions stated in the task	• Must have at least eight questions relevant to the topic being studied • Person chosen for interview must be an "expert" and qualified to provide answers based on product criteria • Questions and answers must be neatly written or typed

Figure 3.2. Product guidelines, continued.

Letter	Map	Mind Map
• Neatly written or typed • Uses proper letter format • At least three paragraphs in length • Must follow type of letter stated in the menu (e.g., friendly, persuasive, informational)	• At least 8.5" by 11" • Accurate information is included • Includes at least 10 relevant locations • Includes compass rose, legend, scale, and key	• At least 8.5" by 11" • Used unlined paper • Must have one central idea • Follow the "no more than four" rule—no more than four words coming from any one word • Should be neatly written or developed using Inspiration
Mobile	**Model**	**Mural**
• At least 10 pieces of related information • Includes color and pictures • At least three layers of hanging information • Hangs in a balanced way	• At least 8" by 8" by 12" • Parts of model must be labeled • Should be in scale when appropriate • Must include a title card • Name should be permanently written on model • $1 contract signed	• At least 22" x 54" • Must contain at least five pieces of important information • Must have colored pictures • Words are optional, but a title should be included • Name should be written on the back in a permanent way
Museum Exhibit	**News Report**	**Newspaper Article**
• Must include at least 10 items • Each item must be labeled • Each item is chosen to specifically meet the needs of the task • Exhibit should fit within the designated space, or is contained in a box • All materials provided should be safe and appropriate for the classroom	• Must address the who, what, where, when, why, and how of the topic. • Script of report turned in with project, or before if performance will be "live" • Must be either performed live or recorded on a VHS tape or DVD	• Must be informational in nature • Must follow standard newspaper format • Must include picture with caption that supports article • At least three paragraphs in length • Neatly written or typed
Paragraph	**Pie Graph**	**Play/Skit**
• Must be neatly written or typed • Must have a topic sentence, at least 3 supporting sentences or details, and a concluding sentence • Must use appropriate vocabulary and follow grammar rules	• Can be created neatly by hand or using computer software • Must have a title • Must have a label for each area or be color coded with a key • Must include the percentages for each area of the graph • Calculations must provided if needed to create the pie graph	• Must be between 5–10 minutes long • Script must be turned in before play is presented • May be presented to an audience or recorded for future showing • Should have props or some form of costume • Can include more than one person

Figure 3.2. Product guidelines, continued.

Poster	PowerPoint—Speaker	PowerPoint—Stand Alone
• Should be the size of a standard poster board • Includes at least five pieces of important information • Must have title • Must contain both words and pictures • Name should be written on the back • Bibliography should be included as needed	• At least 10 informational slides and one title slide with student's name • No more than two words per page • Slides must have color and no more than one graphic per page • Animations are optional but should not distract from information being presented • Presentation should be timed and flow with the speech being given	• At least 10 informational slides and one title slide with student's name • No more than 10 words per page • Slides must have color and no more than one graphic per page • Animation is optional, and must not distract from information being presented
Product Cube	**Puppet**	**Questionnaire**
• All six sides of the cube must be filled with information • Should be neatly written or typed • Name must be printed neatly on the bottom of one of the sides • Should be submitted flat for grading	• Puppet should be handmade and must have a moveable mouth • A list of supplies used to make the puppet will be turned in with the puppet • $1 contract signed • If used in a play, all play criteria must be met as well	• Neatly written or typed • At least 10 questions with possible answers, and at least one answer that requires a written response • Questions must be helpful to gathering information on the topic being studied • At least 15 people must provide answers to questionnaire
Quiz	**Quiz Board**	**Recipe/Recipe Card**
• Must be at least a half sheet of paper • Neatly written or typed • Must cover the specific topic in detail • Must include at least five questions including a short answer question • Must have at least one graphic • An answer key will be turned in with the quiz	• At least five questions • Must have at least five answers • Should use a system with lights to facilitate self-checking • Should be no larger than a poster board • Holiday lights can be used • $1 contract signed	• Must be written neatly or typed on a piece of paper or an index card • Must have a list of ingredients with measurement for each • Must have numbered steps that explain how to make the recipe
Scrapbook	**Song/Rap**	**Speech**
• Cover of scrapbook must have a meaningful title and student's name • Must have at least five themed pages • Each page will have at least one meaningful picture • All photos must have captions	• Words must make sense • Can be presented to an audience or taped • Written words will be turned in before performance or with taped song • Should be at least 2 minutes in length	• Must be at least 2 minutes in length • Should not be read from written paper • Note cards can be used • Written speech must be turned in before speech is presented • Voice must be clear, loud, and easy to understand

Figure 3.2. Product guidelines, continued.

Story	Survey	Three-Dimensional Timeline
• Must have all of the elements of a well-written story (setting, characters, conflict, rising action, and resolution) • Must be appropriate length to allow for story elements • Should be neatly written or typed	• Must have at least five questions related to the topic • Must include at least one adult that is not your teacher • Although the survey writer may fill in the survey form by asking the questions and writing the exact words given by the respondent, the respondent must sign the survey • Information gathered and conclusions drawn from the survey should be written or presented graphically	• Must be no bigger than standard-size poster board • Must be divided into equal time units • Must contain at least 10 important dates and have at least 2 sentences explaining why each date is important • Must have an meaningful, creative object securely attached beside each date to represent that date • Must be able to explain how each object represents each date
Three Facts and a Fib	**Trading Cards**	**Trophy**
• Can be written, typed, or created using Microsoft PowerPoint • Must include exactly four statements: three true statements and one false statement • False statement should not obvious • Brief paragraph should be included that explains why the fib is false	• Include at least 10 cards • Each card should be at least 3" by 5" • Each should have a colored picture • Includes at least three facts on the subject of the card • Cards must have information on both sides • All cards must be submitted in a carrying bag	• Must be at least 6 inches tall • Must have a base with the name of the recipient and the name of the award written neatly or typed on it • Top of trophy must be appropriate and represent the nature of the award • Name should be written on the bottom of the award • Must be an originally designed trophy (avoid reusing a trophy from home)
Venn Diagram	**Video**	**WebQuest**
• At least 8.5" by 11" • Shapes should be thematic and neatly drawn • Must have a title for entire diagram and a title for each section • Must have at least six items in each section of the diagram • Name must be written neatly on the back of the paper	• Use VHS, DVD, or Flash format • Turn in a written plan or story board with project • Students will need to arrange their own video recorder or allow teacher at least 3 days notice for use of video recorder • Covers pertinent information about the project • Name must be written on video label	• Must quest through at least five high-quality Web sites • Web sites should be linked in the document • Can be submitted in a Word or PowerPoint document • At least three questions for each Web site • Must address the topic
Windowpane	**Worksheet**	**You Be the Person Presentation**
• At least 8.5" by 11" unlined paper • At least six squares • Each square must include both a picture and words that should be neatly written or typed • All pictures should be both creative and meaningful • Name should be recorded on the bottom righthand corner of the front of the windowpane	• Must be 8.5" by 11" • Neatly written or typed • Must cover the specific topic or question in detail • Must be creative in design • Must have at least one graphic • An answer key will be turned in with the worksheet	• Take on the role of the person • Cover at least five important facts about the life of the person • Should be between 3 and 5 minutes in length • Script must be turned in before information is presented • Should be presented to an audience with the ability to answer questions while in character • Must have props or some form of costume

Figure 3.2. Product guidelines, continued.

Name:_____ Date:_____

Story Map

Title and Author	Setting

Main Characters
With at Least Three Traits for Each
and a Quote From the Story to Support Each of Your Chosen Traits

Supporting Characters
With One Sentence About Why They Are Important to the Story

Problem

Figure 3.3. Story map.

Name:_____ Date:_____

Major Events in Story

Resolution

Figure 3.3. Story map, continued.

CHAPTER 4

Rubrics

"I frequently end up with more papers and products to grade than with a unit taught in the traditional way. Luckily, the rubric speeds up the process."

—Eighth-grade teacher

The most common reason teachers feel uncomfortable with menus is the need for equal grading. Teachers often feel it is easier to grade the same type of product made by all of the students, rather than grading a large number of different products, none of which looks like any other. The great equalizer for hundreds of different products is a generic rubric that can cover all of the important qualities of an excellent product.

All-Purpose Rubric

Figure 4.1 is an example of a rubric that has been classroom tested with various menus. This rubric can be used with any point value activity presented in a menu. When a menu is presented to students, this rubric can be reproduced on the back of the menu with its guidelines. It also can be given to students to keep in their folder with their product cards so they always know the expectations as they complete products throughout the school year. The first time students see this rubric, it should be explained in detail, especially the last column, Self. It is very important that students self-evaluate their products. This column can provide a unique perspective of the product as it is being graded. *Note*: This rubric was designed to be specific enough that students will know the criteria the teacher is seeking, but general enough that they can still be as creative as they like in the creation of their product. Because all of the point-based menus depend on points that are multiples of 5, the rubric itself has been divided into five areas to make it easier to be more objective with grading.

Student-Taught Lessons and Oral Presentation Rubrics

Although the generic rubric can be used for all activities, there are two occasions that seem to warrant a special rubric: student-taught lessons and oral presentations. These are unique situations, with many fine details that must be considered separately.

Student-taught lessons can cause stress for both students and teachers. Teachers often would like to allow students to teach their fellow classmates, but are not comfortable with the grading aspect of the assignment. Rarely do students understand all of the components that go into designing an effective lesson. This student-taught lesson rubric (see Figure 4.2) helps focus the student on the important aspects of a well-designed lesson and allows teachers to make the evaluation a little more subjective.

One of the focuses of the language arts curriculum is providing opportunities for students to present information in a spoken manner. The oral presentation rubrics assist with this goal. There are two rubrics included: one for the evaluation of the speaker by the teacher (see Figure 4.3) and one for feedback from the students (see Figure 4.4).

Student presentations can be difficult to evaluate. The first consideration is that of objectivity. The objectivity can be addressed through a very specific presentation rubric that states the expectations for the speaker. The rubric will need to be discussed before the students begin preparing presentations and various criteria needs to be demonstrated. The second consideration is that of the audience and its interest. It can be frustrating to have to grade 30 presentations when the audience is not paying attention, off task, or tuning out. This can be solved by allowing your audience to be directly involved in the presentation. All of the students have been

All-Purpose Product Rubric

Name: _____

Criteria	Excellent (Full Credit)	Good (Half Credit)	Poor (No Credit)	Self
Content: Is the content of the product well chosen?	Content chosen represents the best choice for the product. Graphics are well chosen and related to content.	Information or graphics are related to content, but are not the best choice for the product.	Information or graphics presented do not appear to be related to topic or task.	
Completeness: Is everything included in the product?	All information needed is included. Product meets the product criteria and the criteria of the task as stated.	Some important information is missing. Product meets the product criteria and the criteria of the task as stated.	Most important information is missing. The product does not meet the task or does not meet the product criteria.	
Creativity: Is the product original?	Presentation of information is from a new perspective. Graphics are original. Product includes an element of fun and interest.	Presentation of information is from a new perspective. Graphics are not original. Product has elements of fun and interest.	There is no evidence of new thoughts or perspectives in the product.	
Correctness: Is all of the information included correct?	All information presented in the product is correct and accurate.	N/A	Any portion of the information presented in the product is incorrect.	
Communication: Is the information in the product well communicated?	All information is neat and easy to read. Product is in appropriate format and shows significant effort. Oral presentations are easy to understand and presented with fluency.	Most of the product is neat and easy to read. Product is in appropriate format and shows significant effort. Oral presentations are easy to understand, with some fluency.	The product is not neat and easy to read or the product is not in the appropriate format. It does not show significant effort. Oral presentation was not fluent or easy to understand.	
			Total Grade:	

Figure 4.1. All-purpose product rubric.

Student-Taught Lesson Grading Rubric   Name: _____

Parts of Lesson	Excellent	Good	Fair	Poor	Self
Prepared and Ready: All materials and lesson ready at start of class period, from warm-up to conclusion of lesson.	10 Everything is ready to present.	6 Lesson is present, but small amount of scrambling.	3 Lesson is present, but major scrambling.	0 No lesson ready or missing major components.	
Understanding: Presenters understand the material well. Students understand information presented.	20 All information is correct and in correct format.	12 Presenter understands; 25% of students do not.	4 Presenter understands; 50% of students do not.	0 Presenter is confused.	
Complete: Includes all significant information from section or topic.	15 Includes all important information.	10 Includes most important information.	2 Includes less than 50% of the important information.	0 Information is not related.	
Practice: Includes some way for students to practice or access the information.	20 Practice present; well chosen.	10 Practice present; can be applied effectively.	5 Practice present; not related or best choice.	0 No practice or students are confused.	
Interest/Fun: Most of the class was involved, interested, and participating.	15 Everyone interested and participating.	10 75% actively participating.	5 Less than 50% actively participating.	0 Everyone off task.	
Creativity: Information presented in an imaginative way.	20 Wow, creative! I never would have thought of that!	12 Good ideas!	5 Some good pieces but general instruction.	0 No creativity; all lecture, notes, or worksheet.	
				Total Grade:	

Your Topic/Objective:

Comments:

Don't Forget:
All copy requests and material requests must be made at least 24 hours in advance.

Figure 4.2. Student-taught lesson grading rubric.

Oral Presentation Rubric

	Excellent	Good	Fair	Poor	Self
Content—Complete The presentation included everything it should.	**30** Presentation included all of the important information about the topic being presented.	**20** Presentation covered most of the important information, but one key idea was missing.	**10** Presentation covered some of the important information, but more than one key idea was missing.	**0** Presentation included some information, but it was trivial or fluff.	
Content—Correct All of the information presented was accurate.	**30** All of the information presented was accurate.	**20** All of the information presented was correct with a few unintentional errors that were quickly corrected.	**10** Most of the information presented was correct, but there were a few errors.	**0** The information presented was not correct.	
Content—Consistency Speaker stayed on topic during the presentation.	**10** Presenter stayed on topic 100% of the time.	**7** Presenter stayed on topic 90–99% of the time.	**4** Presenter stayed on topic 80–89% of the time.	**0** It was hard to tell what the topic was.	
Prop Speaker had at least one prop that was directly related to the presentation.	**20** Presenter had the prop and it complimented the presentation.	**12** Presenter had a prop, but it was not the best choice.	**4** Presenter had a prop, but there was no clear reason for its choice.	**0** No prop.	
Flow Speaker knew the presentation well, so the words were well-spoken and flowed well together.	**10** Presentation flowed well. Speaker did not stumble over words.	**7** Some flow problems, but they did not distract from information.	**4** Some flow problems interrupted presentation; presenter seemed flustered.	**0** Constant flow problems; information was not presented in a way it could be understood.	
				Total Grade:	

Figure 4.3. Oral presentation rubric.

© Prufrock Press Inc. • *Differentiating With Instruction Menus: Language Arts* • Grades 6–8

This page may be photocopied or reproduced with permission for student use.

39

Topic: _____   Student's Name_____

On a scale of 1–10, rate the following areas:

Content (Depth of information. How well did the speaker know his or her information? Was the information correct? Could the speaker answer questions?)	Your Ranking ☐	Give one specific reason why you gave this number.
Flow (Did the presentation flow smoothly? Did the speaker appear confident and ready to speak?)	Your Ranking ☐	Give one specific reason why you gave this number.
Prop (Did the speaker explain the prop he or she chose? Did the choice seem logical? Was it the best choice?)	Your Ranking ☐	Give one specific reason why you gave this number.

Comments: Below, write two specific things that you think the presenter did well.

- -

Topic: _____   Student's Name_____

On a scale of 1–10, rate the following areas:

Content (Depth of information. How well did the speaker know his or her information? Was the information correct? Could the speaker answer questions?)	Your Ranking ☐	Give one specific reason why you gave this number.
Flow (Did the presentation flow smoothly? Did the speaker appear confident and ready to speak?)	Your Ranking ☐	Give one specific reason why you gave this number.
Prop (Did the speaker explain the prop he or she chose? Did the choice seem logical? Was it the best choice?)	Your Ranking ☐	Give one specific reason why you gave this number.

Comments: Below, write two specific things that you think the presenter did well.

Figure 4.4. Student feedback rubric.

instructed on the oral presentation rubric ahead of time (see Figure 4.3), so when they receive their own rubric to give feedback to their classmates, they are quite comfortable with the criteria. Students are asked to rank their classmates on a scale of 1–10 in the areas of content, flow, and the prop they chose to enhance their presentation (see Figure 4.4). They also are asked to state two things the presenter did well. Although most students understand this should be a positive experience for the presenter, it may want to be reinforced that some notes are not necessary on their peer rankings; for example, if the presenter dropped his or her product and had to pick it up, the presenter knows this and it probably does not need to be noted again. The feedback should be positive and specific. A comment of "Great!" is not what should be recorded; instead, something specific such as, "I could hear you speak loudly and clearly throughout the entire presentation" or "You had great graphics!" should be written on the form. These types of comments really make the students take note and feel great about their presentations. The teacher should not be surprised to note that the students often look through all of their classmates' feedback and comments before ever consulting the rubric the teacher completed. (When used with my students, they actually valued their peers' feedback more than the rubric I gave them with their grades!) Once students have completed a feedback form for a presenter, the forms can then be gathered at the end of each presentation, stapled together, and given to the presenter at the end of the class.

Part 2
The Menus

How to Use the Menu Pages

Each menu in this section has:
- an introduction page for the teacher,
- the content menu,
- any specific guidelines, and
- specific activities mentioned in the menu.

Introduction Pages

The introduction pages are meant to provide an overview of each menu. They are divided into five areas.

1. *Objectives Covered Through the Menu and Activities.* This area will list all of the objectives that the menu can address. Menus are arranged in such a way that if students complete the guidelines set forth in the instructions for the menu, all of these objectives will be covered.

2. *Materials Needed by Students for Completion.* For each menu, it is expected that the teacher will provide, or students will have access to, the following materials: lined paper; glue; crayons, colored pencils, or

markers; and blank 8 ½" by 11" white paper. The introduction page also includes a list of additional materials that may be needed by students. Students do have the choice of which menu items they would like to complete, so it is possible that the teacher will not need all of these materials for every student. Some menu options may involve students developing their own experiment. This will be noted here, as well, with materials commonly used by students in their own experiments.

3. *Special Notes.* Some menus have special management issues or consideration. This section will share any tips to consider for a specific activity or product.

4. *Time Frame.* Each menu has its own ideal Time Frame based on its structure, but all work best with at least a one-week Time Frame. Menus that assess more objectives are better suited to more than 2 weeks. This section will give you an overview about the best Time Frame for completing the entire menu, as well as options for shorter time periods. If teachers do not have time to devote to an entire menu, they certainly can choose the 1–2-day option for any menu topic students are currently studying.

5. *Suggested Forms.* This is a list of the rubrics that should be available for students as the menus are introduced. If a menu has a free-choice option, the appropriate proposal form also will be listed here.

CHAPTER 5

Genres

Biographies

20-50-80 Menu

Reading Objectives Covered Through This Menu and These Activities

- Students will make and explain inferences based on the written work.
- Students will make predictions based on what is read.
- Students will show comprehension by retelling or acting out events in a story.
- Students will show comprehension by summarizing information.
- Students will analyze characters, their relationships, and their importance in the story.
- Students will distinguish between an author's opinion and fact.

Writing Objectives Covered Through This Menu and These Activities

- Students will write to inform, explain, describe, or narrate.
- Students will write to influence or persuade.
- Students will exhibit voice in their writing.

Materials Needed by Students for Completion

- Poster board or large white paper
- Scrapbooking materials
- Materials for three-dimensional timeline

Time Frame

- 1–2 weeks—Students are given the menu as the unit is started, and the teacher discusses all of the product options on the menu. As the different options are discussed, students will choose products that add to a total of 100 points. As the lessons progress through the week(s), the teacher and students refer back to the menu options associated with the content being taught.
- 1–2 days—The teacher chooses an activity or product from the menu to use with the entire class.

Suggested Forms

- All-purpose rubric
- Oral presentation rubric
- Oral presentation feedback form
- Free-choice proposal form for point-based products

Name:_____ Date:_____

Biographies

Directions: Choose two activities from the menu below. The activities must total 100 points. Place a checkmark next to each box to show which activities you will complete. All activities must be completed by _____.

---

20 Points

❏ After reading the biography, choose 10 significant events in the life of the person you read about. Using these dates, create a three-dimensional timeline of his or her life.

❏ Create Three Facts and a Fib about the person in your biography.

---

50 Points

❏ Prepare a "You Be the Person" presentation for your classmates. Be prepared to discuss your life and answer questions from your classmates.

❏ After researching a famous person of your choice, think about the significant events in his or her life. Create a scrapbook about his or her accomplishments.

❏ Design a letter to send to a famous person asking about his or her life and accomplishments. Research the famous person before composing the letter so your questions are relevant. If the person is still alive, send him or her your letter to see if you receive a response.

❏ Free choice—prepare a proposal form and submit your idea for approval.

---

80 Points

❏ Write an autobiography about your life and your accomplishments.

❏ Famous athletes are not the only people who can be on cereal boxes. Design a cereal box based on your own life. Be creative in its design and include a picture, information about the cereal, and a list of your accomplishments.

Graphic Novels

List Menu

Reading Objectives Covered Through This Menu and These Activities

- Students will compare one literary work with another.
- Students will make and explain inferences based on the written work.
- Students will represent textual evidence by using story maps.
- Students will compare different forms of a written work (written versus performed).
- Students will compare one literary genre with another.

Writing Objectives Covered Through This Menu and These Activities

- Students will write to express their feelings, develop ideas, reflect, or problem solve.
- Students will write to inform, explain, describe, or narrate.
- Students will write to influence or persuade.

Materials Needed by Students for Completion

- Poster board or large white paper
- Blank index cards (for trading cards)
- Large lined index cards (for recipe card)
- Internet access (for WebQuest)
- Story map template
- DVD or VHS recorder (for educational video and commercial)
- Materials for three-dimensional timeline

Special Notes on the Use of This Menu

This menu allows students to create a WebQuest. There are multiple versions and templates for WebQuests available on the Internet. Teachers should decide whether to specify a certain format or allow students to create one of their own choosing.

This menu also allows students the opportunity to create an educational video or commercial. Although students enjoy producing their own videos, there often are difficulties obtaining the equipment and scheduling the use of the video recorder. This can be modified by allowing students to act out the educational video or commercial (like a play) or, if students have the technology, they may wish to produce a Webcam or Flash version of their educational video or commercial.

Time Frame

- 1–2 weeks—Students are given the menu as the unit is started and the guidelines and point expectations are discussed. Students usually will need to earn 100 points for 100%, although there is an opportunity for extra credit if the teacher would like to use another target number. Because this menu covers one topic in depth, the teacher will go over all of the options on the menu and have students place checkmarks in the boxes next to the activities they are most interested in completing. Teachers will need to set aside a few moments with each student to sign the agreement at the bottom of the page. As instruction continues, activities are completed by students and submitted for grading.
- 1–2 days—The teacher chooses an activity or product from an objective to use with the entire class during that lesson time.

Suggested Forms

- All-purpose rubric
- Free-choice proposal form for point-based products

Name:_____ Date:_____

Graphic Novels

Guidelines:
1. You may complete as many of the activities listed within the time period.
2. You may choose any combination of activities.
3. Your goal is 100 points. You may earn up to _____ points extra credit.
4. You may be as creative as you like within the guidelines listed below.
5. You must show your plan to your teacher by _____.
6. Activities may be turned in at any time during the working time period. They will be graded and recorded on this sheet as you continue to work, so keep it safe!

Plan to Do	Activity to Complete	Point Value	Date Completed	Points Earned
	Create a Venn diagram that compares and contrasts graphic novels and comic books.	15		
	Design your own graphic novel. Be sure to include all of the elements found in graphic novels.	35		
	After reading an approved graphic novel of your choice, complete a story map for it.	20		
	Write Three Facts and a Fib about the content of your graphic novel.	20		
	Your teacher is not convinced there is educational value in reading graphic novels. Create an educational video about graphic novels and their use in your class.	35		
	Research graphic novels that would be appropriate for your grade level. Make a list of the novels you would recommend to other students.	15		
	Choose a graphic novel that also is a movie or written novel. Create a commercial that compares and contrasts the story and information given in the two formats.	25		
	Create a recipe card that shares the ingredients found in graphic novels and the steps followed in order to write one.	15		
	Design a three-dimensional timeline for the events found in your graphic novel.	20		
	Create a set of trading cards for the characters found in your graphic novel.	15		
	Design a WebQuest that takes questors through the world of graphic novels.	25		
	Free choice—prepare a proposal form and submit your idea for approval.	15–35		
	Total number of points you are planning to earn.		**Total points earned:**	

I am planning to complete _____ activities that could earn up to a total of _____ points.

Teacher's initials _____ Student's signature _____

Name:_____ Date:_____

Story Map

Title and Author	Setting

Main Characters
With at Least Three Traits for Each
and a Quote From the Story to Support Each of Your Chosen Traits

Supporting Characters
With One Sentence About Why They Are Important to the Story

Problem

Name:_____ Date:_____

Major Events in Story

Resolution

Nonfiction

20-50-80 Menu

Reading Objectives Covered Through This Menu and These Activities

- Students will compare one written work with another.
- Students will use resources and references to build meaning.
- Students will share information gained from reading a nonfiction selection.
- Students will evaluate the information provided in nonfiction sources.

Writing Objectives Covered Through This Menu and These Activities

- Students will write to express their feelings, develop ideas, reflect, or problem solve.
- Students will write to inform, explain, describe, or narrate.
- Students will write to influence or persuade.

Materials Needed by Students for Completion

- Poster board or large white paper
- Graph paper or Internet access (for crossword puzzle)
- Microsoft PowerPoint or other slideshow software
- Magazines (for collage)

Time Frame

- 1–2 weeks—Students are given the menu as the unit is started, and the teacher discusses all of the product options on the menu. As the different options are discussed, students will choose products that add to a total of 100 points. As the lessons progress through the week(s), the teacher and students refer back to the menu options associated with the content being taught.
- 1–2 days—The teacher chooses an activity or product from the menu to use with the entire class.

Suggested Forms

- All-purpose rubric
- Free-choice proposal form for point-based products

Nonfiction

Directions: Choose two activities from the menu below. The activities must total 100 points. Place a checkmark next to each box to show which activities you will complete. All activities must be completed by _____.

---

20 Points

❑ Create a collage of pictures related to your topic.

❑ Design a PowerPoint presentation to share information about your topic.

---

50 Points

❑ Use facts from your nonfiction selection to create a museum exhibit. Include a written description of the objects or photos.

❑ Write a song or rap to help teach others about your topic. It needs to include at least 10 details about your topic.

❑ Create a brochure that shares important details about your topic, why you chose it, and how it relates to your everyday life.

❑ Design a crossword puzzle with information provided in the nonfiction book you selected.

---

80 Points

❑ Choose two different nonfiction books about your topic. After reading each book, determine which you feel is the better book. Design a book cover for that book. In the editorial comments area, include your reasons for choosing it.

❑ Free choice—prepare a proposal form and submit your idea for approval.

Novel Study

Tic-Tac-Toe Menu

Reading Objectives Covered Through This Menu and These Activities

- Students will make predictions based on what is read.
- Students will show comprehension by summarizing a story.
- Students will analyze characters, their relationships, and their importance in the story.
- Students will recognize and analyze story plot and problem resolution.

Writing Objectives Covered Through This Menu and These Activities

- Students will write to express their feelings, develop ideas, reflect, or problem solve.
- Students will support their responses with textual evidence.
- Students will write to inform, explain, describe, or narrate.
- Students will write to influence or persuade.
- Students will exhibit voice in their writing.

Materials Needed by Students for Completion

- Poster board or large white paper
- Cube template
- DVD or VHS recorder (for video and commercial)
- Materials for three-dimensional timeline

Special Notes on the Use of This Menu

This menu allows students the opportunity to create a video or commercial. Although students enjoy producing their own videos, there often are difficulties obtaining the equipment and scheduling the use of the video recorder. This can be modified by allowing students to act out the video or commercial (like a play) or, if students have the technology, they may wish to produce a Webcam or Flash version of their video or commercial.

Time Frame

- 2–3 weeks—Students are given the menu as the unit is started. As the teacher presents lessons throughout the week, he or she should refer back to the menu options associated with that content. The teacher will go over all of the options for that content and have students place checkmarks in the boxes that represent the activities they are most interested in completing. As teaching continues over the next 2–3 weeks, activities chosen and completed should make a column or row. When students complete this pattern, they have completed one activity from each content area, learning style, or level of Bloom's, depending on the design of the menu.

- 1 week—At the start of the unit, the teacher chooses the three activities he or she feels are most valuable for the students. Stations can be set up in the classroom. These three activities are available for student choice throughout the week as regular instruction takes place.
- 1–2 days—The teacher chooses an activity from the menu to use with the entire class.

Suggested Forms

- All-purpose rubric
- Oral presentation rubric
- Oral presentation feedback form
- Free-choice proposal form

Name:_____ Date:_____

Novel Study

☐ *Character Analysis* Choose a character other than the main character that you feel had a significant impact on the story. Design a "You Be the Person" presentation in which you come to class as your character and talk about your impact on the plot and theme of your novel.	☐ *Promoting Your Novel* Consider all of the reasons your classmates might enjoy reading your novel. Create an advertisement to encourage your classmates to read your novel. Make it unique and interesting!	☐ *Proving Your Point* Complete this statement with just one word: Everyone thinks the main character of my novel is _____. Create a cube with the six best quotes from your novel that prove your statement is true. Be sure to document where each quote was found.
☐ *Proving Your Point* Determine the theme of your novel. Choose at least four quotes from your novel that strongly support the theme and at least four quotes that neither support nor disprove it. Create a folded quiz book that asks users to determine if the quotes support the theme.	☐ **Free Choice: Character Analysis** (Fill out your proposal form before beginning the free choice!)	☐ *Promoting Your Novel* There are various reasons why people choose the novels they would like to read, from the cover, to the summary on the back cover, to the recommendations of other people. Create a persuasive commercial that shares all of this information about your novel.
☐ *Promoting Your Novel* The Book Hall of Fame is taking nominations for the best fiction book ever written. Create a nomination video for your book. Describe your book and why it deserves the honor.	☐ *Proving Your Point* Create a game show that has contestants evaluating quotes from your novel and determining if they support given statements about it.	☐ *Character Analysis* Create a three-dimensional timeline for the main character in your novel. Include at least one date before the novel begins.

Check the boxes you plan to complete. They should form a tic-tac-toe across or down.
All products are due by: _____.

Novel Study Cube

After determining the best adjective to complete the sentence, "Everyone thinks my main character is _____," place a quote from the story on each side of the cube to support the word you chose. Include where each quote was found in your novel. Use this pattern or create your own cube.

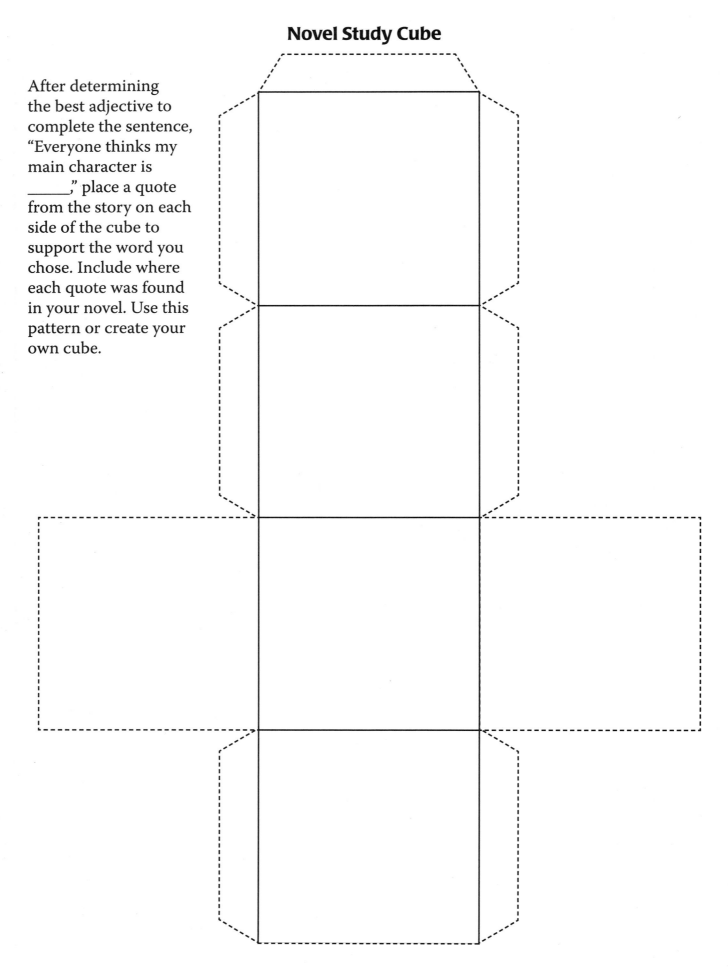

Plays

Tic-Tac-Toe Menu

Reading Objectives Covered Through This Menu and These Activities

- Students will show comprehension by retelling or acting out events in a story.
- Students will show comprehension by summarizing a story.
- Students will compare different forms of a written work (written versus performed).
- Students will compare one literary genre with another.
- Students will recognize and analyze story plot and problem resolution.

Writing Objectives Covered Through This Menu and These Activities

- Students will write to express their feelings, develop ideas, reflect, or problem solve.
- Students will write to inform, explain, describe, or narrate.
- Students will write to entertain.
- Students will write to influence or persuade.
- Students will exhibit voice in their writing.
- Students will use vivid language.
- Students will revise drafts.

Materials Needed by Students for Completion

- Poster board or large white paper
- Socks (for puppets)
- Paper bags (for puppets)

Time Frame

- 2–3 weeks—Students are given the menu as the unit is started. As the teacher presents lessons throughout the week, he or she should refer back to the menu options associated with that content. The teacher will go over all of the options for that content and have students place checkmarks in the boxes that represent the activities they are most interested in completing. As teaching continues over the next 2–3 weeks, activities chosen and completed should make a column or row. When students complete this pattern, they have completed one activity from each content area, learning style, or level of Bloom's, depending on the design of the menu.

- 1 week—At the start of the unit, the teacher chooses the three activities he or she feels are most valuable for the students. Stations can be set up in the classroom. These three activities are available for student choice throughout the week as regular instruction takes place.
- 1–2 days—The teacher chooses an activity from the menu to use with the entire class.

Suggested Forms

- All-purpose rubric
- Oral presentation rubric
- Oral presentation feedback form
- Free-choice proposal form

Name: _____ Date: _____

Plays

☐ *Evaluating Your Play* Create an advertisement to promote your play. Be sure to include the aspects of your play that you found most interesting to persuade others to read it.	☐ *Create Your Own Play* Choose one of your favorite fictional stories. Convert this story into a play.	☐ *Compare Your Play* Choose a play that you have seen performed either on television or in person. Design a mind map that compares and contrasts the written version to the performance.
☐ *Compare Your Play* After reading a play, convert it into children's book. Design a book cover for your book. Include editorial comments that explain how the play and the children's book are similar and different.	☐ ***Free Choice: Evaluating Your Play*** (Fill out your proposal form before beginning the free choice!)	☐ *Create Your Own Play* Make an original puppet show with at least two characters to share with your classmates.
☐ *Create Your Own Play* Create your own dramatic play that you can perform for your classmates.	☐ *Compare Your Play* After choosing a play that you have both read and seen performed, write Three Facts and a Fib that compare and contrast your written play to the one that was performed.	☐ *Evaluating Your Play* Read a play of your choice. Write a newspaper review that expresses your thoughts about the quality of the play and why you feel this way.

Check the boxes you plan to complete. They should form a tic-tac-toe across or down.
All products are due by: _____.

Poetry

List Menu

Reading Objectives Covered Through This Menu and These Activities

- Students will interpret figurative language and multiple meaning words.
- Students will use resources and references to build meaning.

Writing Objectives Covered Through This Menu and These Activities

- Students will write to express their feelings, develop ideas, and reflect.
- Students will write to inform, explain, describe, or narrate.
- Students will write to entertain.
- Students will write to influence or persuade.
- Students will exhibit voice in their writing.
- Students will use vivid language.
- Students will revise drafts.

Materials Needed by Students for Completion

- Poster board or large white paper
- Internet access (for WebQuest)
- Materials for bulletin board display

Special Notes on the Use of This Menu

This menu allows students to create a bulletin board display. Some classrooms may only have one bulletin board, so the teacher can divide the board into sections, or additional classroom wall or hall space can be sectioned off for the creation of these displays. Students can plan their display based on the amount of space they are assigned.

This menu also allows students to create a WebQuest. There are multiple versions and templates for WebQuests available on the Internet. Teachers should decide whether to specify a certain format or allow students to create one of their own choosing.

Time Frame

- 1–2 weeks—Students are given the menu as the unit is started and the guidelines and point expectations are discussed. Students usually will need to earn 100 points for 100%, although there is an opportunity for extra credit if the teacher would like to use another target number. Because this menu covers one topic in depth, the teacher will go over all of the options on the menu and have students place checkmarks in the boxes next to the activities they are most interested in completing. Teachers will need to set aside a few moments with each student to sign the agreement at the bottom of the page. As instruction continues, activities are completed by students and submitted for grading.

- 1–2 days—The teacher chooses an activity or product from an objective to use with the entire class during that lesson time.

Suggested Forms

- All-purpose rubric
- Free-choice proposal form for point-based products

Name:_____ Date:_____

Poetry

Guidelines:

1. You may complete as many of the activities listed within the time period.
2. You may choose any combination of activities.
3. Your goal is 100 points. You may earn up to _____ points extra credit.
4. You may be as creative as you like within the guidelines listed below.
5. You must show your plan to your teacher by _____.
6. Activities may be turned in at any time during the working time period. They will be graded and recorded on this sheet as you continue to work, so keep it safe!

Plan to Do	Activity to Complete	Point Value	Date Completed	Points Earned
	Create a brochure about poetry, the different types of poems, and the various reasons people write them.	20		
	Choose one of your favorite poems and transform it into a song or rap. Be prepared to share your creation with your classmates.	15		
	Create your own children's book of poetry with at least five poems you have written.	30		
	Research the history of the haiku poem. Make a poster that shows your research, as well as three examples of this type of poem.	15		
	Write and perform a play in which two original poems you have written have an important part.	30		
	Create a book of poetry with examples from at least three different poetry types (e.g., diamante, cinquain, haiku, name poem, free verse, etc.)	15		
	Research poems that have been banned for cultural reasons. Choose one and create a poster about the poem. State the reasons for being banned and your opinions on these reasons.	25		
	After choosing your favorite book of poetry, design a book cover for it.	20		
	Design a WebQuest that takes questors through various examples of poetry, both old and new, allowing them to read and evaluate the poems.	30		
	Create a bulletin board display that shows the impact poetry can have on its readers. Include examples of various poems.	25		
	Choose a poem from one of Shel Silverstein's poetry books. Create your own drawing or illustration for the poem you choose.	20		
	Free choice—prepare a proposal form and submit your idea for approval.	15–30		
	Total number of points you are planning to earn.	**Total points earned:**		

I am planning to complete _____ activities that could earn up to a total of _____ points.

Teacher's initials _____ Student's signature _____

Science Fiction

Tic-Tac-Toe Menu

Reading Objectives Covered Through This Menu and These Activities

- Students will make and explain inferences based on the written work.
- Students will show comprehension by retelling or acting out events in a story.
- Students will show comprehension by summarizing a story.
- Students will analyze characters, their relationships, and their importance in the story.
- Students will recognize and analyze story plot and problem resolution.

Writing Objectives Covered Through This Menu and These Activities

- Students will write to express their feelings, develop ideas, reflect, or problem solve.
- Students will write to inform, explain, describe, or narrate.
- Students will write to entertain.
- Students will write to influence or persuade.
- Students will exhibit voice in their writing.

Materials Needed by Students for Completion

- Poster board or large white paper
- Coat hangers (for mobile)
- Index cards (for mobile)
- String (for mobile)
- Ruler (for comic strip or cartoon)
- DVD or VHS recorder (for commercial and news report)
- Materials for board games (folders, colored cards, etc.)
- Story map template

Special Notes on the Use of This Menu

This menu allows students the opportunity to create a commercial or news report. Although students enjoy producing their own videos, there often are difficulties obtaining the equipment and scheduling the use of the video recorder. This can be modified by allowing students to act out the commercial or news report (like a play) or, if students have the technology, they may wish to produce a Webcam or Flash version of their commercial or news report.

Time Frame

- 2–3 weeks—Students are given the menu as the unit is started. As the teacher presents lessons throughout the week, he or she should refer back to the menu options associated with that content. The teacher will go over all of the options for that content and have students place checkmarks in the boxes that represent the activities they are most interested in completing. As teaching continues over the next 2–3 weeks, activities chosen and completed should make a column or row. When students complete this pattern, they have completed one activity from each content area, learning style, or level of Bloom's, depending on the design of the menu.
- 1 week—At the start of the unit, the teacher chooses the three activities he or she feels are most valuable for the students. Stations can be set up in the classroom. These three activities are available for student choice throughout the week as regular instruction takes place.
- 1–2 days—The teacher chooses an activity from the menu to use with the entire class.

Suggested Forms

- All-purpose rubric
- Oral presentation rubric
- Oral presentation feedback form
- Free-choice proposal form

Name: _____ Date: _____

Science Fiction

□ *Share It!*	□ *Live It!*	□ *Make It Mobile!*
After reading your selection, determine the most important aspects of the plot and rewrite your selection as a children's book.	Choose the scene from your book that you feel had the greatest impact on the plot. Reenact this scene from your book in a play. Be sure to design appropriate costumes!	Consider the elements necessary for a written work to be considered science fiction. Create a mobile that shows all of the elements of your science fiction selection.
□ *Draw It!*	□ **Free Choice: Your Science Fiction Selection**	□ *Advertise It!*
Identify your favorite science fiction character and show his or her next adventure using a cartoon format. Be creative; include a new setting and adventure for your character.	(Fill out your proposal form before beginning the free choice!)	Create a commercial for an item or invention used in your reading selection that does not exist in our time or has been changed significantly.
□ *Document It!*	□ *Play With It!*	□ *Write It!*
Science fiction novels often are filled with lots of drama or action. Create a news report that documents the most important event in your selection.	After reading your science fiction selection, create a board game with that theme. Be sure your board game incorporates quotes about your characters and their traits as well as their impact on the plot.	Write your own science fiction story set in the future. Include a story map that shows your prewriting, as well as your rough draft.

Check the boxes you plan to complete. They should form a tic-tac-toe across or down.
All products are due by: _____.

Story Map

Title and Author	Setting

Main Characters
With at Least Three Traits for Each
and a Quote From the Story to Support Each of Your Chosen Traits

Supporting Characters
With One Sentence About Why They Are Important to the Story

Problem

Major Events in Story

Resolution

© Prufrock Press Inc. • *Differentiating With Instruction Menus: Language Arts* • *Grades 6–8*

This page may be photocopied or reproduced with permission for student use.

69

Fiction

Baseball Menu

Reading Objectives Covered Through This Menu and These Activities

- Students will compare one literary work with another.
- Students will interpret figurative language and multiple meaning words.
- Students will make and explain inferences based on the written work.
- Students will make predictions based on what is read.
- Students will show comprehension by retelling or acting out events in a story.
- Students will show comprehension by summarizing a story.
- Students will represent textual evidence by using story maps.
- Students will analyze characters, their relationships, and their importance in the story.
- Students will recognize and analyze story plot and problem resolution.

Writing Objectives Covered Through This Menu and These Activities

- Students will write to express their feelings, develop ideas, reflect, or problem solve.
- Students will support their responses with textual evidence.
- Students will write to inform, explain, describe, or narrate.
- Students will write to entertain.
- Students will write to influence or persuade.
- Students will exhibit voice in their writing.
- Students will use vivid language.

Materials Needed by Students for Completion

- Poster board or large white paper
- Story map template
- Magazines (for collage)
- Materials for board games (folders, colored cards, etc.)
- Ruler (for comic strip)
- Coat hangers (for mobile)
- Index cards (for mobile)
- String (for mobile)
- Microsoft PowerPoint or other slideshow software
- DVD or VHS recorder (for news report)
- Materials for creating trophy

Special Notes on the Use of This Menu

This menu allows students the opportunity to create a news report. Although students enjoy producing their own videos, there often are difficulties obtaining the equipment and scheduling the use of the video recorder. This can be modified by allowing students to act out the news report (like a play) or, if students have the technology, they may wish to produce a Webcam or Flash version of their news report.

Time Frame

- 2–3 weeks—Students are given the menu as the unit is started and the guidelines and point expectations on the top of the menu are discussed. Usually, students are expected to complete 100 points. Because this menu covers one topic in depth, the teacher will go over all of the options for the topic being covered and have students place checkmarks in the boxes next to the activities they are most interested in completing. As instruction continues, activities are completed by students and submitted for grading.
- 1 week—At the beginning of the unit, the teacher chooses 1–2 higher level activities that can be integrated into whole-group instruction throughout the week.
- 1–2 days—The teacher chooses an activity from an objective to use with the entire class during that lesson time.

Suggested Forms

- All-purpose rubric
- Oral presentation rubric
- Oral presentation feedback form
- Free-choice proposal form for point-based projects

Name:_____ Date:_____

Fiction

Look through the following choices and decide how you want to make your game add to 100 points. Singles are worth 10, doubles are worth 30, triples are worth 50, and a home run is worth 100. Choose any combination you want. Place a checkmark next to each choice you are going to complete. Make sure that your points equal 100!

If you are using this menu for more than one book, please write the titles and authors of the books you are using below:

1. _____

2. _____

3. _____

4. _____

Singles—10 Points Each

❏ Fill in a story map for a fictional story of your choice.

❏ Create a quiz that covers the plot, themes, and characters in your book.

❏ Create a book cover for your story or novel.

❏ Design a personality collage for two of your favorite characters from the story or novel (they do not have to be the main characters). The collage should contain at least 20 words for each character.

❏ Create a diorama of your favorite scene in the story or novel.

❏ Write a folded quiz book about the characters and events in your story or novel.

❏ Create a three-dimensional timeline that shows the major events in your story or novel.

❏ Using a Venn diagram, compare and contrast two different books written by the author of your story or novel.

Doubles—30 Points Each

❏ Design an acrostic for your favorite character. Use character traits for each letter of his or her name. Choose two quotes from the story or novel to support the traits you choose.

❏ Design an advertisement for your book that encourages your classmates to read it.

❏ Create a board game to follow the events in your story or novel.

❏ The author of your book is contemplating allowing his or her characters to be used in a new comic strip. Design the comic strip.

❏ Design a greeting card you could give one of your characters for something he or she experienced during the story or novel.

❏ We often wish we knew what the future holds in store for each of us. Write a letter to one of your characters early in the book, giving him or her advice that would help that character in the near future.

Doubles, continued

❏ Create a character mobile. Place all of your characters on the mobile with two traits for each one. Under each trait, select a quote from the book that supports why you chose that trait.

❏ Create a news report that explains the resolution in your story or novel.

❏ Create a windowpane with at least 10 panes for the theme of your book. Place quotes from different parts of the story or novel in each pane that exemplify how the theme is seen throughout the work.

Triples—50 Points

❏ The Book Hall of Fame is taking nominations for the best book best ever written. Design a PowerPoint presentation to submit a book for this honor. Describe your book in detail and why it deserves the honor.

❏ Consider the theme, characters, and plot of your book. Write a children's book that uses the same theme, characters, or plot (choose only one of the three). Do not just retell the story—make it creative!

❏ Two of the characters in your story or novel have been selected as contestants on a local game show. Invent a game show in which they could participate, taking into consideration their abilities and strengths. Perform your game show.

Home Run—100 Points

❏ Two of your characters have been nominated for a special award. Taking into consideration their strengths and good deeds, determine what type of award this might be. Although both characters may not qualify, define and record the criteria for the award and design a trophy for the award. Using PowerPoint, create a submission application for both characters that documents their personality traits and achievements (both stated and unstated) that makes them qualified for the award. Be sure to support each achievement or personality trait with a quote from the novel or story. Based on the criteria, select the winner and perform his or her acceptance speech.

I Chose:

_____Singles (10 points each)

_____Doubles (30 points each)

_____Triples (50 points each)

_____Home Run (100 points)

Name:_____ Date:_____

Story Map

Title and Author	Setting

Main Characters
With at Least Three Traits for Each
and a Quote From the Story to Support Each of Your Chosen Traits

Supporting Characters
With One Sentence About Why They Are Important to the Story

Problem

Major Events in Story

Resolution

CHAPTER 6

Novels

The Dark Is Rising

List Menu

Synopsis

On his 11th birthday, Will Stanton, seventh son of a seventh son, finds his world has suddenly changed. Early on his birthday morning, Will awakes to find himself centuries back in time and discovers that he is actually the last of the "Old Ones," a mystical group whose mission has always been to keep the forces of the Dark under control. Will has been born with a great gift of power, and he now must undertake the heroic quest to find and to join together the six Signs of the Light—for "the Dark is rising."

Reading Objectives Covered Through This Menu and These Activities

- Students will make and explain inferences based on the written work.
- Students will make predictions based on what is read.
- Students will show comprehension by retelling or acting out events in a story.
- Students will show comprehension by summarizing a story.
- Students will represent textual evidence by using story maps.
- Students will compare different forms of a written work (written versus performed).
- Students will analyze characters, their relationships, and their importance in the story.
- Students will recognize and analyze story plot and problem resolution.

Writing Objectives Covered Through This Menu and These Activities

- Students will write to express their feelings, develop ideas, and reflect.
- Students will support their responses with textual evidence.
- Students will write to inform, explain, describe, or narrate.
- Students will write to entertain.
- Students will write to influence or persuade.

Materials Needed by Students for Completion

- *The Dark Is Rising* by Susan Cooper
- Poster board or large white paper
- Story map template
- Magazines (for collage)
- Microsoft PowerPoint or other slideshow software

- DVD or VHS recorder (for news report)
- Internet access (for WebQuest)

Special Notes on the Use of This Menu

This menu allows students to create a WebQuest. There are multiple versions and templates for WebQuests available on the Internet. Teachers should decide whether to specify a certain format or allow students to create one of their own choosing.

This menu also allows students the opportunity to create a news report. Although students enjoy producing their own videos, there often are difficulties obtaining the equipment and scheduling the use of the video recorder. This can be modified by allowing students to act out the news report (like a play) or, if students have the technology, they may wish to produce a Webcam or Flash version of their news report.

Time Frame

- 1–2 weeks—Students are given the menu as the unit is started and the guidelines and point expectations are discussed. Students usually will need to earn 100 points for 100%, although there is an opportunity for extra credit if the teacher would like to use another target number. Because this menu covers one topic in depth, the teacher will go over all of the options on the menu and have students place checkmarks in the boxes next to the activities they are most interested in completing. Teachers will need to set aside a few moments with each student to sign the agreement at the bottom of the page. As instruction continues, activities are completed by students and submitted for grading.
- 1–2 days—The teacher chooses an activity or product from an objective to use with the entire class during that lesson time.

Suggested Forms

- All-purpose rubric
- Oral presentation rubric
- Oral presentation feedback form
- Free-choice proposal form for point-based products

Name:_____ Date:_____

The Dark Is Rising

Guidelines:
1. You may complete as many of the activities listed within the time period.
2. You may choose any combination of activities.
3. Your goal is 100 points. You may earn up to _____ points extra credit.
4. You may be as creative as you like within the guidelines listed below.
5. You must show your plan to your teacher by _____.
6. Activities may be turned in at any time during the working time period. They will be graded and recorded on this sheet as you continue to work, so keep it safe!

Plan to Do	Activity to Complete	Point Value	Date Completed	Points Earned
	Complete a story map for *The Dark Is Rising*.	15		
	Design an advertisement for one of the signs of light and its value to the "Old Ones."	20		
	Weather plays a big part in the advancement of the Dark in this book. Create Three Facts and a Fib about these weather changes and the weather conditions usually found in Britain.	20		
	Design a game show about *The Dark Is Rising* in which players answer questions while trying to obtain and join the signs of light together.	35		
	This book also has been released as a movie. After reading the book, watch the movie and create a Venn diagram that shares their similarities and differences. Include a paragraph that states which format you enjoyed more and why.	35		
	Will has been considered a hero. Write and perform a speech in which he discusses his thoughts about being considered a hero by others.	30		
	Will lives in a rectory. Investigate his surroundings and create a diorama of his home.	25		
	Create a collage of modern-day items that are examples of the different signs of light.	20		
	Create a book cover for *The Dark Is Rising*.	20		
	Investigate different types of fractals, including those used in this book. Create a PowerPoint presentation that shares pictures as examples.	25		
	Create a folded quiz book for the different people Will encounters on his journey.	20		
	Create a news report that shares the consequences for the world if Will cannot attain his goal.	35		
	Free choice—prepare a proposal form and submit your idea for approval.	15–35		
	Total number of points you are planning to earn.	**Total points earned:**		

I am planning to complete _____ activities that could earn up to a total of _____ points.

Teacher's initials _____ Student's signature _____

Name:_____ Date:_____

Story Map

Title and Author	Setting

Main Characters
With at Least Three Traits for Each
and a Quote From the Story to Support Each of Your Chosen Traits

Supporting Characters
With One Sentence About Why They Are Important to the Story

Problem

Name:_____ Date:_____

Major Events in Story

Resolution

Julie of the Wolves

Tic-Tac-Toe Menu

Synopsis

After her father is suspected dead, Miyax, a 13-year-old Eskimo girl, finds herself forced into an arranged marriage. The marriage is not a happy one and after a frightening comment, she decides to run away to San Francisco, where she is known as Julie. Unfortunately, she runs out of supplies during her trip from Alaska to San Francisco and is in a dire situation. It is then that she meets a wolf pack, which, after many encounters, accepts her as one of its own. Living with the wolves helps her reevaluate her culture, its ways, and the ways of the humans who hunt animals for sport. After growing to love the wolves, she hears her father may not be dead. Should she return to him and live that life, or should she remain in the wild with her new beloved family, the wolves?

Reading Objectives Covered Through This Menu and These Activities
- Students will make and explain inferences based on the written work.
- Students will make predictions based on what is read.
- Students will show comprehension by retelling or acting out events in a story.
- Students will show comprehension by summarizing a story.
- Students will analyze characters, their relationships, and their importance in the story.
- Students will recognize and analyze story plot and problem resolution.

Writing Objectives Covered Through This Menu and These Activities
- Students will write to express their feelings, develop ideas, reflect, or problem solve.
- Students will write to inform, explain, describe, or narrate.
- Students will write to entertain.

Materials Needed by Students for Completion
- *Julie of the Wolves* by Jean Craighead George
- Poster board or large white paper
- Internet access (for WebQuest)
- DVD or VHS recorder (for educational video and news report)
- Scrapbooking materials
- Microsoft PowerPoint or other slideshow software

Special Notes on the Use of This Menu

This menu allows students to create a WebQuest. There are multiple versions and templates for WebQuests available on the Internet. Teachers should decide whether to specify a certain format or allow students to create one of their own choosing.

This menu also allows students the opportunity to create an educational video or news report. Although students enjoy producing their own videos, there often are difficulties obtaining the equipment and scheduling the use of the video recorder. This can be modified by allowing students to act out the educational video or news report (like a play) or, if students have the technology, they may wish to produce a Webcam or Flash version of their educational video or news report.

Time Frame

- 2–3 weeks—Students are given the menu as the unit is started. As the teacher presents lessons throughout the week, he or she should refer back to the menu options associated with that content. The teacher will go over all of the options for that content and have students place checkmarks in the boxes that represent the activities they are most interested in completing. As teaching continues over the next 2–3 weeks, activities chosen and completed should make a column or row. When students complete this pattern, they have completed one activity from each content area, learning style, or level of Bloom's, depending on the design of the menu.
- 1 week—At the start of the unit, the teacher chooses the three activities he or she feels are most valuable for the students. Stations can be set up in the classroom. These three activities are available for student choice throughout the week as regular instruction takes place.
- 1–2 days—The teacher chooses an activity from the menu to use with the entire class.

Suggested Forms

- All-purpose rubric
- Oral presentation rubric
- Oral presentation feedback form
- Free-choice proposal form

Name:_____ Date:_____

Julie of the Wolves

☐ **The Tundra** Create a WebQuest that takes questors through the traditions of Eskimos, the lives of wolves, and the state of Alaska.	☐ **Julie's Life** Choose the 10 most important days in Julie's life. Create a diary with entries for each of these days. With each entry, include a drawing that Julie may have sketched.	☐ **Julie and the Wolves** After making her final choice, the television station you work for has decided to interview her about her life and her decision. Perform a news report sharing the information you gather during the interview.
☐ **Julie and the Wolves** Choose one of Julie's days with the wolves that you found meaningful. Rewrite the experience to take place between humans rather than wolves. Perform your experience as a play for your classmates.	☐ **Free Choice: Eskimos, Wolves, and Alaska** (Fill out your proposal form before beginning the free choice!)	☐ **Julie's Life** Design a scrapbook that documents Julie's life from the time her mother died until she makes her final decision.
☐ **Julie's Life** As a newspaper reporter, you have been sent to interview Julie about her life and the events that had the greatest impact on how she now lives. Create an interview for Julie and provide her responses.	☐ **Julie and the Wolves** Julie was able to survive with the wolves because she came to understand how they were similar to humans in certain ways. Create an educational video that shows the similarities and differences between wolves and humans.	☐ **The Tundra** Create a stand-alone PowerPoint presentation that provides information on Eskimos and their traditions, the geography of Alaska, and the behaviors of wolves found there.

Check the boxes you plan to complete. They should form a tic-tac-toe across or down.

All products are due by: _____.

© Prufrock Press Inc. • *Differentiating With Instruction Menus: Language Arts* • Grades 6–8

This page may be photocopied or reproduced with permission for student use.

85

The True Confessions of Charlotte Doyle

20-50-80 Menu

Synopsis

On a long, adventure-filled journey from England to Rhode Island in 1802, 13-year-old Charlotte changes from the prim and proper girl her parents want her to be to part of a mutinous crew aboard the *Seahawk*. Can she survive the trip as the only female on board—and did she really murder someone?

Reading Objectives Covered Through This Menu and These Activities

- Students will make and explain inferences based on the written work.
- Students will make predictions based on what is read.
- Students will show comprehension by retelling or acting out events in a story.
- Students will show comprehension by summarizing a story.
- Students will analyze characters, their relationships, and their importance in the story.
- Students will recognize and analyze story plot and problem resolution.

Writing Objectives Covered Through This Menu and These Activities

- Students will support their responses with textual evidence.
- Students will write to express their feelings, develop ideas, reflect, or problem solve.
- Students will write to inform, explain, describe, or narrate.
- Students will write to entertain.
- Students will write to influence or persuade.

Materials Needed by Students for Completion

- *The True Confessions of Charlotte Doyle* by Avi
- Poster board or large white paper
- Magazines (for collage)
- Materials for board games (folders, colored cards, etc.)
- Microsoft PowerPoint or other slideshow software
- DVD or VHS recorder (for news report)

Special Notes on the Use of This Menu

This menu allows students the opportunity to create a news report. Although students enjoy producing their own videos, there often are difficulties obtaining the equipment and scheduling the use of the video recorder. This can be modified by allowing students to act out the news report (like a play) or, if students have the technology, they may wish to produce a Webcam or Flash version of their news report.

Time Frame

- 1–2 weeks—Students are given the menu as the unit is started, and the teacher discusses all of the product options on the menu. As the different options are discussed, students will choose products that add to a total of 100 points. As the lessons progress through the week(s), the teacher and students refer back to the menu options associated with the content being taught.
- 1–2 days—The teacher chooses an activity or product from the menu to use with the entire class.

Suggested Forms

- All-purpose rubric
- Oral presentation rubric
- Oral presentation feedback form
- Free-choice proposal form for point-based projects

The True Confessions of Charlotte Doyle

Directions: Choose two activities from the menu below. The activities must total 100 points. Place a checkmark next to each box to show which activities you will complete. All activities must be completed by _____.

---

20 Points

❏ Create Three Facts and a Fib about Charlotte's journey.

❏ Design a collage divided in half that represents Charlotte's personality before and after the trip.

---

50 Points

❏ Create a poster that compares and contrasts the jobs available to women in 1800 and the jobs open to women now.

❏ Design a brochure that explains how to be a proper, well-mannered young woman (by 1800 standards), as well as how to be an effective shipmate.

❏ Make a board game in which players take a part in Charlotte's adventures.

❏ Free choice—prepare a proposal form and submit your idea for approval.

---

80 Points

❏ Design a PowerPoint presentation with slides for the different sailors on the ship, as well as Captain Jaggery and Charlotte. Include information about each character and your impressions about their names, which were carefully chosen by the author. Include at least one quote from the book for each character to defend your descriptive statements.

❏ Write and perform a news report that documents the trial of Charlotte Doyle.

The Face on the Milk Carton

Tic-Tac-Toe Menu

Synopsis

Janie is just an average teenager until the day she sees a picture on her milk container of a kidnapped young girl in a polka-dotted dress. She is certain she is that young girl. After some investigation on her own, culminating with finding the same polka-dotted dress in the attic, she finally confronts her parents about her suspicions. Did her loving parents kidnap her?

Reading Objectives Covered Through This Menu and These Activities

- Students will make and explain inferences based on the written work.
- Students will make predictions based on what is read.
- Students will show comprehension by retelling or acting out events in a story.
- Students will show comprehension by summarizing a story.
- Students will analyze characters, their relationships, and their importance in the story.
- Students will recognize and analyze story plot and problem resolution.

Writing Objectives Covered Through This Menu and These Activities

- Students will write to express their feelings, develop ideas, reflect, or problem solve.
- Students will support their responses with textual evidence.
- Students will write to inform, explain, describe, or narrate.

Materials Needed by Students for Completion

- *The Face on the Milk Carton* by Caroline B. Cooney
- Poster board or large white paper
- DVD or VHS recorder (for news report)
- Scrapbooking materials
- Microsoft PowerPoint or other slideshow software
- Blank index cards (for trading cards)

Special Notes on the Use of This Menu

This menu allows students the opportunity to create a news report. Although students enjoy producing their own videos, there often are difficulties obtaining the equipment and scheduling the use of the video recorder. This can be modified by allowing students to act out the news report (like a play) or, if students have the technology, they may wish to produce a Webcam or Flash version of their news report.

Time Frame

- 2–3 weeks—Students are given the menu as the unit is started. As the teacher presents lessons throughout the week, he or she should refer back to the menu options associated with that content. The teacher will go over all of the options for that content and have students place checkmarks in the boxes that represent the activities they are most interested in completing. As teaching continues over the next 2–3 weeks, activities chosen and completed should make a column or row. When students complete this pattern, they have completed one activity from each content area, learning style, or level of Bloom's, depending on the design of the menu.
- 1 week—At the start of the unit, the teacher chooses the three activities he or she feels are most valuable for the students. Stations can be set up in the classroom. These three activities are available for student choice throughout the week as regular instruction takes place.
- 1–2 days—The teacher chooses an activity from the menu to use with the entire class.

Suggested Forms

- All-purpose rubric
- Oral presentation rubric
- Oral presentation feedback form
- Free-choice proposal form

Name:_____ Date:_____

The Face on the Milk Carton

☐ **The Key Players** Create a flipbook about the different characters found in the book. Include a written description and drawing of each person. Include at least two quotes for each character to support your written description and drawing.	☐ **Now What?** You are a newspaper reporter who has been sent to speak with Janie about her experiences. Create a news report in which you interview Janie and find out what she plans to do next.	☐ **Finding Herself** Janie's world turned upside down that day in the cafeteria. Create a scrapbook that documents Janie's road to the discovery of her true identity.
☐ **Finding Herself** List all of the discoveries Janie makes that led her to her true identity. Create a PowerPoint presentation that places these discoveries in order of importance to Janie.	☐ **Free Choice: Characters Found in the Book** (Fill out your proposal form before beginning the free choice!)	☐ **Now What?** Thinking about how the book ended, what do you think Janie will do next? Write the epilogue in story form that follows her next steps.
☐ **Now What?** Write and perform a play that documents the next few months of Janie's life following the ending of the book.	☐ **Finding Herself** Teenagers struggle with finding their identity, and Janie's struggle was even more significant. Create a journal entry for each day that she made a new discovery in her quest to find her true identity.	☐ **The Key Players** Create a set of trading cards for the characters found in *The Face on the Milk Carton*. Include at least one quote about each person that supports your statements about his or her personality.

Check the boxes you plan to complete. They should form a tic-tac-toe across or down.
All products are due by: _____.

The Giver

20-50-80 Menu

Synopsis

Jonas lives in a community that is safe, predictable, and planned. People rarely need to make choices; there is no sadness or despair, no sunshine or cold, no music, and no animals. Everyone understands and follows the order of the community, including pursuing the profession they are assigned. Jonas finds himself assigned to be the Receiver of Memories. He will have access to the memories of the past—when the community was different, when there was sorrow and pain, but also choice. The more memories Jonas receives, the more he questions his community. Should he continue to accept it or try to change it?

Reading Objectives Covered Through This Menu and These Activities

- Students will prove conclusions using textual evidence.
- Students will make and explain inferences based on the written work.
- Students will make predictions based on what is read.
- Students will show comprehension by retelling or acting out events in a story.
- Students will show comprehension by summarizing a story.
- Students will represent textual evidence by using story maps.
- Students will analyze characters, their relationships, and their importance in the story.
- Students will recognize and analyze story plot and problem resolution.

Writing Objectives Covered Through This Menu and These Activities

- Students will support their responses with textual evidence.
- Students will write to inform, explain, describe, or narrate.
- Students will write to influence or persuade.
- Students will exhibit voice in their writing.

Materials Needed by Students for Completion

- *The Giver* by Lois Lowry
- Coat hangers (for mobile)
- Index cards (for mobile)
- String (for mobile)
- Story map template
- Scrapbooking materials

Time Frame

- 1–2 weeks—Students are given the menu as the unit is started, and the teacher discusses all of the product options on the menu. As the different options are discussed, students will choose products that add to a total of 100 points. As the lessons progress through the week(s), the teacher and students refer back to the menu options associated with the content being taught.
- 1–2 days—The teacher chooses an activity or product from the menu to use with the entire class.

Suggested Forms

- All-purpose rubric
- Student-taught lesson rubric
- Free-choice proposal form for point-based projects

The Giver

Directions: Choose two activities from the menu below. The activities must total 100 points. Place a checkmark next to each box to show which activities you will complete. All activities must be completed by _____.

---

20 Points

❏ Design a mobile with the characters found in *The Giver* and their traits. Include quotes from the book to support the traits you have chosen for each.

❏ Complete a story map for *The Giver*.

---

50 Points

❏ Create a children's book about someone your age who tries to change his or her neighborhood into a perfect community.

❏ Write an essay that describes your perfect world. Include what makes it so perfect.

❏ Create an informational brochure for the community assignment you think best fits your skills.

❏ Free choice—prepare a proposal form and submit your idea for approval.

---

80 Points

❏ There are many ways that we accumulate and maintain memories of our past, from photographs in scrapbooks to oral storytelling and videotapes. You have been given the task of maintaining the memories of the American people from the Mayflower until now. After choosing your method for maintaining the memories, create a sample set of "memories" from a time period of your choice.

❏ Design a class lesson that allows your classmates to experience how colors and music can evoke different emotions.

Name:_____ Date:_____

Story Map

Title and Author	Setting

Main Characters
With at Least Three Traits for Each
and a Quote From the Story to Support Each of Your Chosen Traits

Supporting Characters
With One Sentence About Why They Are Important to the Story

Problem

Major Events in Story

Resolution

The Outsiders

Tic-Tac-Toe Menu

Synopsis

This story follows the experiences of Ponyboy and his fellow Greasers as they encounter the Socs, a rival gang. After getting caught speaking to two girlfriends of the Socs, Ponyboy and Johnny are jumped in the park. In order to stop one of the Socs from drowning Ponyboy, Johnny stabs him. This makes things even worse for between the groups, so Johnny and Ponyboy flee to a church to hide. While there, they end up setting the church on fire while there are elementary students present. Ponyboy and Johnny could easily escape but the children would be in danger. Should they run? Should they help? If they do help, what might be the consequences?

Reading Objectives Covered Through This Menu and These Activities

- Students will make and explain inferences based on the written work.
- Students will make predictions based on what is read.
- Students will show comprehension by retelling or acting out events in a story.
- Students will show comprehension by summarizing a story.
- Students will analyze characters, their relationships, and their importance in the story.
- Students will recognize and analyze story plot and problem resolution.

Writing Objectives Covered Through This Menu and These Activities

- Students will write to express their feelings, develop ideas, reflect, or problem solve.
- Students will write to inform, explain, describe, or narrate.
- Students will write to influence or persuade.
- Students will exhibit voice in their writing.

Materials Needed by Students for Completion

- *The Outsiders* by S. E. Hinton
- Poster board or large white paper
- Blank index cards (for trading cards)
- Microsoft PowerPoint or other slideshow software
- DVD or VHS recorder (for news report)
- *Gone With the Wind* by Margaret Mitchell
- Materials for three-dimensional timeline

Special Notes on the Use of This Menu

This menu allows students the opportunity to create a news report. Although students enjoy producing their own videos, there often are difficulties obtaining the equipment and scheduling the use of the video recorder. This can be modified by allowing students to act out the news report (like a play) or, if students have the technology, they may wish to produce a Webcam or Flash version of their news report.

Time Frame

- 2–3 weeks—Students are given the menu as the unit is started. As the teacher presents lessons throughout the week, he or she should refer back to the menu options associated with that content. The teacher will go over all of the options for that content and have students place checkmarks in the boxes that represent the activities they are most interested in completing. As teaching continues over the next 2–3 weeks, activities chosen and completed should make a column or row. When students complete this pattern, they have completed one activity from each content area, learning style, or level of Bloom's, depending on the design of the menu.
- 1 week—At the start of the unit, the teacher chooses the three activities he or she feels are most valuable for the students. Stations can be set up in the classroom. These three activities are available for student choice throughout the week as regular instruction takes place.
- 1–2 days—The teacher chooses an activity from the menu to use with the entire class.

Suggested Forms

- All-purpose rubric
- Oral presentation rubric
- Oral presentation feedback form
- Student-taught lesson rubric
- Free-choice proposal form

Name:_____ Date:_____

The Outsiders

☐ **The Events** Choose the 10 events you think had the greatest impact on the plot of the story. Create a three-dimensional timeline for these events.	☐ **A New Ending** Choose one scene in the novel that you would like to rewrite to impact the ending of the book. Rewrite and perform your newly revised scene as a play.	☐ **The Characters** Create two sets of trading cards for all of the characters in the rival groups—one set for all of the Socs and one set for the Greasers.
☐ **The Characters** Choose the character in the story that you identify with the most. Develop a "You Be the Person" presentation in which you come to class as that character and discuss your life and relationships with the other characters.	☐ **Free Choice: Events in The Outsiders** (Fill out your proposal form before beginning the free choice!)	☐ **Gone With the Wind** The book *Gone With the Wind* was important to Ponyboy. Create a PowerPoint presentation that shares the plot of and characters in this book by Margaret Mitchell. Include your thoughts on why Ponyboy identified so strongly with this book.
☐ **Say It in Song** Choose several songs that you think reflect the feelings of characters as they change throughout the book. Put the songs together to create an audio collage. Provide a paragraph for each song that explains why it was chosen.	☐ **The Characters** Although not Greasers themselves, Cherry and Marcia have an impact on the future of the Greasers. Create at least 10 diary entries that document events in the story and share their impressions of all of the characters.	☐ **The Events** Choose one of the most important events in the story and create a news report to describe it. Your report should be in the format of a live "breaking news" interview.

Check the boxes you plan to complete. They should form a tic-tac-toe across or down.
All products are due by: _____.

Anne Frank: The Diary of a Young Girl

List Menu

Synopsis

Anne Frank and her family members found themselves in a situation where they needed to go into hiding during the reign of the Nazis in World War II. This book documents their 2-year stay in the Secret Annex as they try to stay hidden from the Nazis.

Reading Objectives Covered Through This Menu and These Activities

- Students will prove conclusions using textual evidence.
- Students will make and explain inferences based on the written work.
- Students will make predictions based on what is read.
- Students will show comprehension by retelling or acting out events in a story.
- Students will show comprehension by summarizing a story.
- Students will recognize and analyze story plot and problem resolution.

Writing Objectives Covered Through This Menu and These Activities

- Students will support their responses with textual evidence.
- Students will write to inform, explain, describe, or narrate.
- Students will write to influence or persuade.
- Students will exhibit voice in their writing.

Materials Needed by Students for Completion

- Poster board or large white paper
- Microsoft PowerPoint or other slideshow software
- Materials for model
- Internet access (for WebQuest)
- Magazines (for collage)

Special Notes on the Use of This Menu

This menu allows students to create a WebQuest. There are multiple versions and templates for WebQuests available on the Internet. Teachers should decide whether to specify a certain format or allow students to create one of their own choosing.

Time Frame

- 1–2 weeks—Students are given the menu as the unit is started and the guidelines and point expectations are discussed. Students usually will need to earn 100 points for 100%, although there is an opportunity for extra credit if the teacher would like to use another target number. Because this menu covers one topic in depth, the teacher will go over all of the options on the menu and have students place checkmarks in the boxes next to the activities they are most interested in completing. Teachers will need to set aside a few moments with each student to sign the agreement at the bottom of the page. As instruction continues, activities are completed by students and submitted for grading.
- 1–2 days—The teacher chooses an activity or product from an objective to use with the entire class during that lesson time.

Suggested Forms

- All-purpose rubric
- Free-choice proposal form for point-based products

Name:_____ Date:_____

Anne Frank: The Diary of a Young Girl

Guidelines:
1. You may complete as many of the activities listed within the time period.
2. You may choose any combination of activities.
3. Your goal is 100 points. You may earn up to _____ points extra credit.
4. You may be as creative as you like within the guidelines listed below.
5. You must show your plan to your teacher by _____.
6. Activities may be turned in at any time during the working time period. They will be graded and recorded on this sheet as you continue to work, so keep it safe!

Plan to Do	Activity to Complete	Point Value	Date Completed	Points Earned
	Make a list of at least 10 different emotions Anne Frank experiences during her stay in the Secret Annex. Design a PowerPoint presentation of the emotions, with examples of when she experiences each and at least one quote that shows each emotion.	30		
	Create a cross-cut model of the building that contained the Secret Annex.	25		
	Write Three Facts and a Fib about Anne's stay in the Secret Annex.	20		
	Design a WebQuest that takes questors through information about the Holocaust. Please choose sites that are more informational in nature and appropriate for all ages.	30		
	There are various reasons why people may need to go into hiding. Create a brochure that explains what is needed to go into hiding and how to not draw attention to you or your family. Base your ideas on the Frank family's experience.	25		
	Gather statistics about the Holocaust and create a pie graph that shows your findings.	15		
	Make a three-dimensional timeline that documents Anne Frank's stay in the Secret Annex, as well as at least two dates before she entered into the Annex and two dates after she left.	25		
	There were things that Anne Frank and her family did without in the Annex. Create a collage of items that would have made their stay easier.	20		
	Design a book cover for the diary of Anne Frank.	15		
	Create a worksheet for the story elements found in *Anne Frank: The Diary of a Young Girl.*	20		
	Write a newspaper article about the events that led to the Holocaust and why Hitler made the decisions he did.	25		
	Free choice—prepare a proposal form and submit your idea for approval.	15–30		
	Total number of points you are planning to earn.	**Total points earned:**		

I am planning to complete _____ activities that could earn up to a total of _____ points.

Teacher's initials _____ Student's signature _____

Flowers for Algernon

20-50-80 Menu

Synopsis

Charlie is a happy man who is learning disabled. He enjoys his work and the life he has made for himself. He is offered the opportunity to undergo an experimental surgical procedure that could greatly increase his intelligence. After the procedure, he makes incredible progress as his intelligence increases and his experiences change. Soon after, however, the mouse that received the surgery before Charlie begins to show signs of returning to its original intellect. Will the same thing happen to Charlie, and if so, how will he accept the change?

Reading Objectives Covered Through This Menu and These Activities

- Students will make and explain inferences based on the written work.
- Students will make predictions based on what is read.
- Students will show comprehension by retelling or acting out events in a story.
- Students will show comprehension by summarizing a story.
- Students will represent textual evidence by using story maps.
- Students will recognize and analyze story plot and problem resolution.

Writing Objectives Covered Through This Menu and These Activities

- Students will support their responses with textual evidence.
- Students will write to inform, explain, describe, or narrate.
- Students will write to influence or persuade.

Materials Needed by Students for Completion

- *Flowers for Algernon* by Daniel Keyes
- DVD or VHS recorder (for infomercial)
- Story map template

Special Notes on the Use of This Menu

This menu allows students the opportunity to create an infomercial. Although students enjoy producing their own videos, there often are difficulties obtaining the equipment and scheduling the use of the video recorder. This can be modified by allowing students to act out the infomercial (like a play) or, if students have the technology, they may wish to produce a Webcam or Flash version of their infomercial.

Time Frame

- 1–2 weeks—Students are given the menu as the unit is started, and the teacher discusses all of the product options on the menu. As the different options are discussed, students will choose products that add to a total of 100 points. As the lessons progress through the week(s), the teacher and students refer back to the menu options associated with the content being taught.
- 1–2 days—The teacher chooses an activity or product from the menu to use with the entire class.

Suggested Forms

- All-purpose rubric
- Oral presentation rubric
- Oral presentation feedback form
- Free-choice proposal form for point-based projects

Flowers for Algernon

Directions: Choose two activities from the menu below. The activities must total 100 points. Place a checkmark next to each box to show which activities you will complete. All activities must be completed by _____.

---

20 Points

❏ Create a brochure about intelligence and how it is measured.

❏ Create Three Facts and a Fib about the abilities and characteristics of highly intelligent people.

---

50 Points

❏ Pretend that Charlie's surgery had been a success. Design an infomercial for this new surgical opportunity and its potential impact on society.

❏ Create a children's book about intelligence and accepting yourself as you are. Use examples from *Flowers for Algernon* in your story.

❏ Complete a story map for *Flowers for Algernon*.

❏ Free choice—prepare a proposal form and submit your idea for approval.

---

80 Points

❏ Contemplate the role that Algernon played in this novel. Write and perform a play of *Flowers for Algernon* from the viewpoint of Algernon rather than Charlie.

❏ If you had the same opportunity as Charlie—to increase your intelligence significantly—but perhaps lose it and yet remember you once had it, would you still elect to have the surgery? Write a newspaper article that shares your feelings.

Name:_____ Date:_____

Story Map

Title and Author	Setting

Main Characters
With at Least Three Traits for Each
and a Quote From the Story to Support Each of Your Chosen Traits

Supporting Characters
With One Sentence About Why They Are Important to the Story

Problem

Major Events in Story

Resolution

Nothing but the Truth

List Menu

Synopsis

Philip, a typical ninth grader, discovers he will not be eligible to participate in the track team thanks to a teacher who "gave him" a failing grade on a test. When he later gets transferred into her homeroom class, he finds a way to annoy her by humming the "Star-Spangled Banner" when it is supposed to be quiet. When he gets in trouble, it gets blown completely out of proportion when the media catches wind of the story. How far can this issue be taken? Is it really a civic issue of freedom?

Reading Objectives Covered Through This Menu and These Activities

- Students will prove conclusions using textual evidence.
- Students will make and explain inferences based on the written work.
- Students will make predictions based on what is read.
- Students will show comprehension by retelling or acting out events in a story.
- Students will show comprehension by summarizing a story.
- Students will analyze characters, their relationships, and their importance in the story.
- Students will recognize and analyze story plot and problem resolution.

Writing Objectives Covered Through This Menu and These Activities

- Students will write to express their feelings.
- Students will support their responses with textual evidence.
- Students will write to inform, explain, describe, or narrate.
- Students will write to influence or persuade.
- Students will exhibit voice in their writing.

Materials Needed by Students for Completion

- *Nothing but the Truth* by Avi
- Large lined index cards (for instruction card)
- Internet access (for WebQuest)
- DVD or VHS recorder (for news report)
- Microsoft PowerPoint or other slideshow software

Special Notes on the Use of This Menu

This menu allows students to create a WebQuest. There are multiple versions and templates for WebQuests available on the Internet. Teachers should decide whether to specify a certain format or allow students to create one of their own choosing.

This menu also allows students the opportunity to create a news report. Although students enjoy producing their own videos, there often are difficulties obtaining the equipment and scheduling the use of the video recorder. This can be modified by allowing students to act out the news report (like a play) or, if students have the technology, they may wish to produce a Webcam or Flash version of their news report.

Time Frame

- 1–2 weeks—Students are given the menu as the unit is started and the guidelines and point expectations are discussed. Students usually will need to earn 100 points for 100%, although there is an opportunity for extra credit if the teacher would like to use another target number. Because this menu covers one topic in depth, the teacher will go over all of the options on the menu and have students place checkmarks in the boxes next to the activities they are most interested in completing. Teachers will need to set aside a few moments with each student to sign the agreement at the bottom of the page. As instruction continues, activities are completed by students and submitted for grading.
- 1–2 days—The teacher chooses an activity or product from an objective to use with the entire class during that lesson time.

Suggested Forms

- All-purpose rubric
- Oral presentation rubric
- Oral presentation feedback form
- Free-choice proposal form for point-based products

Name:_____ Date:_____

Nothing but the Truth

Guidelines:
1. You may complete as many of the activities listed within the time period.
2. You may choose any combination of activities.
3. Your goal is 100 points. You may earn up to _____ points extra credit.
4. You may be as creative as you like within the guidelines listed below.
5. You must show your plan to your teacher by _____.
6. Activities may be turned in at any time during the working time period. They will be graded and recorded on this sheet as you continue to work, so keep it safe!

Plan to Do	Activity to Complete	Point Value	Date Completed	Points Earned
	Reenact the scene in which Philip hums along to the "Star-Spangled Banner," but create a different ending that could have solved the problem immediately.	35		
	Philip was upset by his low grade on his test. Create an instruction card that lists other options he has to obtain a better grade next time. Be as specific as possible.	15		
	This title has different meanings when considering all the ways truth is exploited throughout the book. Create a speech that explains what the phrase "nothing but the truth" really means to you.	35		
	Design a WebQuest that investigates the concept of freedom and its importance to humankind.	25		
	Watch at least half an hour of the nightly news. Create a news report about how the media (or news) impacts people.	30		
	Create a "You Be the Person" presentation in which you come to school as Miss (Mr.) Narwin and discuss your decision.	25		
	Write a biased news article entitled "Suspended for Humming" in which you are in favor of the suspension.	30		
	Create a PowerPoint presentation in which you share at least 10 different examples of how truth impacts this story. Include quotes that show how each one impacted the plot.	30		
	Create Three Facts and a Fib about Philip.	20		
	The ending of this book is full of irony. Create a worksheet that explains irony using examples and quotes from the book.	20		
	Create a "What would you do if you were Miss Narwin or Philip?" survey. Present your information on a poster.	25		
	Write the next chapter in the book. Be sure to address what happens to all of the main characters involved.	30		
	Free choice—prepare a proposal form and submit your idea for approval.	15–35		
	Total number of points you are planning to earn.		**Total points earned:**	

I am planning to complete _____ activities that could earn up to a total of _____ points.

Teacher's initials _____ Student's signature _____

The Odyssey

20-50-80 Menu

Synopsis

This epic poem follows the journey of Odysseus as he tries to return home after the Trojan War, as well as the happenings that have taken place in his absence. The play is filled with adventure and creative solutions to the problems he faces.

Reading Objectives Covered Through This Menu and These Activities

- Students will prove conclusions using textual evidence.
- Students will make and explain inferences based on the written work.
- Students will make predictions based on what is read.
- Students will show comprehension by retelling or acting out events in a story.
- Students will show comprehension by summarizing a story.
- Students will represent textual evidence by using story maps.
- Students will recognize and analyze story plot and problem resolution.

Writing Objectives Covered Through This Menu and These Activities

- Students will support their responses with textual evidence.
- Students will write to inform, explain, describe, or narrate.

Materials Needed by Students for Completion

- Poster board or large white paper
- Story map template
- Cube template
- Materials for board games (folders, colored cards, etc.)
- Scrapbooking materials

Special Notes on the Use of This Menu

Students also are given the opportunity to create a game for the class. The length of the game is not stated in the product guidelines, so the teacher can determine what works best. It may be good to have students start with shorter games and work up to longer games with a review focus.

Time Frame

- 1–2 weeks—Students are given the menu as the unit is started, and the teacher discusses all of the product options on the menu. As the different options are discussed, students will choose products that add to a total of 100 points. As the lessons progress through the week(s), the teacher and students refer back to the menu options associated with the content being taught.

• 1–2 days—The teacher chooses an activity or product from the menu to use with the entire class.

Suggested Forms

• *The Odyssey* by Homer
• All-purpose rubric
• Oral presentation rubric
• Oral presentation feedback form
• Free-choice proposal form for point-based projects

Name:_____ Date:_____

The Odyssey

Directions: Choose two activities from the menu below. The activities must total 100 points. Place a checkmark next to each box to show which activities you will complete. All activities must be completed by _____.

---

20 Points

❏ Complete a story map for *The Odyssey*.

❏ Create a story cube for *The Odyssey*.

---

50 Points

❏ Create a board game that allows players to experience the adventures Odysseus encounters during *The Odyssey*.

❏ Design a class game that quizzes your classmates on the plot developments, characters, and their traits found in *The Odyssey*.

❏ Develop a scrapbook for Odysseus and his travels. Be sure to decorate each page using a theme appropriate to that adventure.

❏ Free choice—prepare a proposal form and submit your idea for approval.

---

80 Points

❏ *The Odyssey* is an epic poem filled with many short adventures. Choose the adventure that you think best shows Odysseus' heroic traits and create a children's book for it.

❏ Odysseus had many, varied experiences in his travels. Determine the adventure that is the best example of Odysseus displaying his cunning and problem-solving skills. Create a "You Be the Person" presentation in which you come to class as Odysseus. Be ready to discuss this adventure and the way you used your cunning.

The Odyssey Cube

Use this cube to share the different aspects of *The Odyssey*.

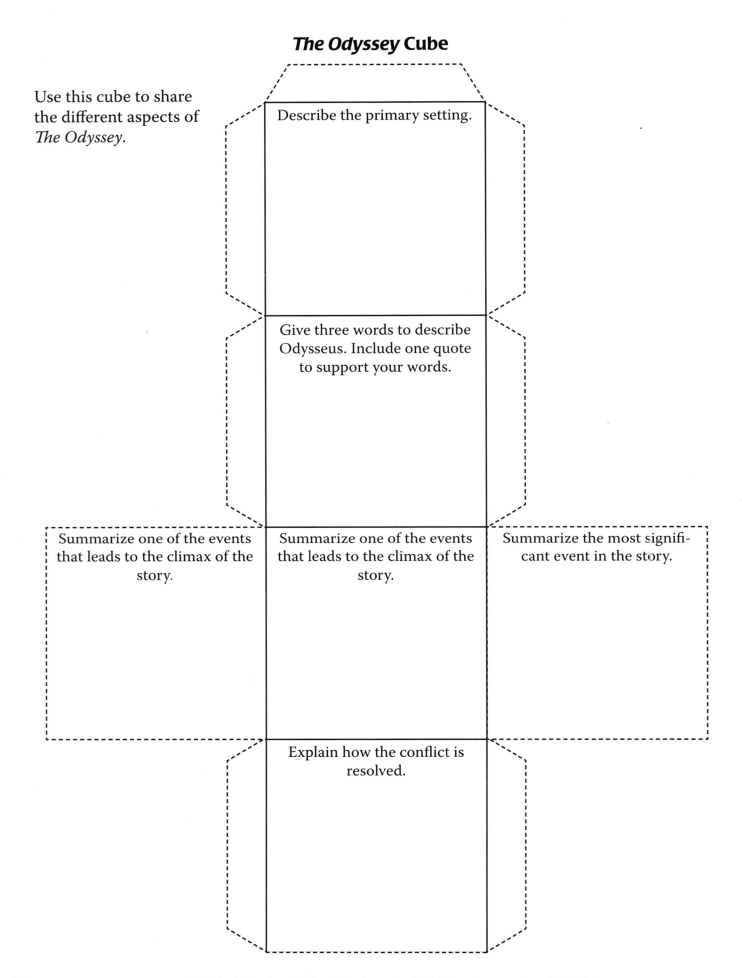

Describe the primary setting.

Give three words to describe Odysseus. Include one quote to support your words.

Summarize one of the events that leads to the climax of the story.

Summarize one of the events that leads to the climax of the story.

Summarize the most significant event in the story.

Explain how the conflict is resolved.

Name:_____ Date:_____

Story Map

Title and Author	Setting

Main Characters
With at Least Three Traits for Each
and a Quote From the Story to Support Each of Your Chosen Traits

Supporting Characters
With One Sentence About Why They Are Important to the Story

Problem

Name:_____ Date:_____

Major Events in Story

Resolution

Author Study

Tic-Tac-Toe Menu

Reading Objectives Covered Through This Menu and These Activities
- Students will compare one literary work with another.
- Students will make and explain inferences based on the written work.
- Students will make predictions based on what is read.
- Students will compare different forms of a written work (written versus performed).
- Students will analyze characters, their relationships, and their importance in the story.
- Students will distinguish between an author's opinion and fact.
- Students will recognize and analyze story plot and problem resolution.

Writing Objectives Covered Through This Menu and These Activities
- Students will write to express their feelings, develop ideas, reflect, or problem solve.
- Students will write to inform, explain, describe, or narrate.
- Students will write to entertain.
- Students will write to influence or persuade.
- Students will exhibit voice in their writing.
- Students will use vivid language.

Materials Needed by Students for Completion
- Poster board or large white paper
- Materials for bulletin board display
- Microsoft PowerPoint or other slideshow software
- Aluminum foil (for quiz board)
- Materials for three-dimensional timeline

Special Notes on the Use of This Menu
This menu allows students to create a bulletin board display. Some classrooms may only have one bulletin board, so the teacher can divide the board into sections, or additional classroom wall or hall space can be sectioned off for the creation of these displays. Students can plan their display based on the amount of space they are assigned.

Time Frame

- 2–3 weeks—Students are given the menu as the unit is started. As the teacher presents lessons throughout the week, he or she should refer back to the menu options associated with that content. The teacher will go over all of the options for that content and have students place checkmarks in the boxes that represent the activities they are most interested in completing. As teaching continues over the next 2–3 weeks, activities chosen and completed should make a column or row. When students complete this pattern, they have completed one activity from each content area, learning style, or level of Bloom's, depending on the design of the menu.
- 1 week—At the start of the unit, the teacher chooses the three activities he or she feels are most valuable for the students. Stations can be set up in the classroom. These three activities are available for student choice throughout the week as regular instruction takes place.
- 1–2 days—The teacher chooses an activity from the menu to use with the entire class.

Suggested Forms

- All-purpose rubric
- Free-choice proposal form

Name:_____ Date:_____

Author Study

☐ *The Author's Life* Create a three-dimensional timeline of the significant events in your author's life that led to his or her career in writing.	☐ *The Author's Works* Write an original play in which at least three different characters from three different books by your author meet and have an adventure. If your author has written only one or two books, use characters from those.	☐ *The Author's Peers* Choose an author who writes with a purpose similar to your author. Create a greeting card that the other author might send to your author congratulating him or her on his or her newest novel.
☐ *The Author's Peers* Create a bulletin board display about your author and other authors that you feel have a similar vision or purpose. Your display should focus on the similarities between your author and the others you have chosen.	☐ ***Free Choice: The Author's Life*** (Fill out your proposal form before beginning the free choice!)	☐ *The Author's Works* Design a game show that quizzes contestants on the similarities and differences of characters, themes, plots, and the author's purpose found in various examples of your author's work.
☐ *The Author's Works* After reading different works written by your author, compose a letter that shares your feelings about his or her specific works and what you felt your author's purpose was when writing each. Locate the address of your author's publisher and send the letter to your author.	☐ *The Author's Peers* Choose another author whom you feel writes in a way similar to your author. Create a PowerPoint presentation that shows similarities in his or her choice of characters, themes, plots, and purpose.	☐ *The Author's Life* Consider the events in your author's life that have had the greatest impact on his or her works and writing style. Write a newspaper article about the life and writing career of your author.

Check the boxes you plan to complete. They should form a tic-tac-toe across or down.
All products are due by: _____.

CHAPTER 7

Writing and Mechanics

Self- and Peer Editing

List Menu

Reading Objectives Covered Through This Menu and These Activities
- Students will read, analyze, and critique their own writing and that of their peers.

Writing Objectives Covered Through This Menu and These Activities
- Students will support their responses with textual evidence.
- Students will provide constructive criticism and suggestions for improvements to their writing.
- Students will suggest how to exhibit voice in their writing.
- Students will revise drafts.

Materials Needed by Students for Completion
- Colored pencils (preferably not red) for editing suggestions

Time Frame
- 1–2 days—Students are given this menu in order to facilitate self- and peer editing. It can be given before the writing process begins so students will know what others will be looking for when editing or after the first draft has been created. The students can read the paper and then choose how they would like to edit it.

Suggested Forms
- All-purpose rubric
- Free-choice proposal form for point-based products

Name:_____ Date:_____

Self- and Peer Editing

Guidelines:
1. You must have finished your writing assignment before beginning this menu.
2. You may choose any combination of editing strategies.
3. Your goal is 50 points. You may earn up to _____ points extra credit.
4. You must show your plan to your teacher by _____.
5. Keep in mind that the editing comments should be *positive* and *constructive* in nature.

Plan to Do	Activity to Complete	Point Value	Date Completed	Points Earned
	Check the paper for proper spelling and capitalization.	5		
	Check commas and quotation marks to be sure they are used properly.	5		
	Check the paper to be sure all of the sentences are complete, with no fragments or run-ons.	10		
	Check for overused words and circle them.	10		
	Evaluate the vocabulary used in the assignment and suggest at least three more precise words that could replace weaker words currently being used.	10		
	Check the assignment for any off-topic sentences or information. Mark the information and note why it seems to be off topic.	10		
	As you read, write at least two more questions about what you are reading that could help improve the writing. Write your questions next to the paragraph to which they relate.	10		
	Locate and mark at least one sentence that could be made better by adding additional detail and suggest some of those details.	10		
	Read the assignment aloud to a classmate and ask for two specific suggestions on how to make it better. Note the suggestions at the bottom of the assignment.	15		
	Check the assignment for proper paragraph structure. Does it follow the assigned structure? If so, provide a positive comment about the structure. If not, provide a constructive comment to help improve the structure.	15		
	Comment on what you think is the best part of the assignment. Your comment should be specific and constructive.	15		
	If appropriate, locate and comment on the use of voice in the writing. If voice is not present, but could be, provide constructive ideas on how to integrate it.	15		
	Read the paper beginning at the end, one sentence at a time, to double-check for grammatical errors. Make at least two suggestions for improving the paper.	15		
	Free choice—prepare a proposal form and submit your idea for approval.	5–15		
	Total number of points you are planning to earn.		**Total points earned:**	

I am planning to complete _____ activities that could earn up to a total of _____ points.

Teacher's initials _____ Student's signature _____

Vocabulary Skills

Tic-Tac-Toe Menu

Reading Objectives Covered Through This Menu and These Activities

- Students will use resources and references to build meaning.
- Students will interpret figurative language and multiple meaning words.

Writing Objectives Covered Through This Menu and These Activities

- Students will write to express their feelings, develop ideas, reflect, or problem solve.
- Students will write to inform, explain, describe, or narrate.
- Students will write to entertain.
- Students will write to influence or persuade.
- Students will exhibit voice in their writing.
- Students will use vivid language.

Materials Needed by Students for Completion

- Poster board or large white paper
- Graph paper or Internet access (for crossword puzzle)
- Blank index cards (for trading cards)
- Aluminum foil (for quiz board)
- Wires (for quiz board)

Special Notes on the Use of This Menu

Students also are given the opportunity to create a game for the class. The length of the game is not stated in the product guidelines, so the teacher can determine what works best. It may be good to have students start with shorter games and work up to longer games with a review focus.

Time Frame

- 2–3 weeks—Students are given the menu as the unit is started. As the teacher presents lessons throughout the week, he or she should refer back to the menu options associated with that content. The teacher will go over all of the options for that content and have students place checkmarks in the boxes that represent the activities they are most interested in completing. As teaching continues over the next 2–3 weeks, activities chosen and completed should make a column or row. When students complete this pattern, they have completed one activity from each content area, learning style, or level of Bloom's, depending on the design of the menu.

- 1 week—At the start of the unit, the teacher chooses the three activities he or she feels are most valuable for the students. Stations can be set up in the classroom. These three activities are available for student choice throughout the week as regular instruction takes place.
- 1–2 days—The teacher chooses an activity from the menu to use with the entire class.

Suggested Forms

- All-purpose rubric
- Oral presentation rubric
- Oral presentation feedback form
- Free-choice proposal form

Name:_____ Date:_____

Vocabulary Skills

☐ *Design a Greeting Card*	☐ *Prepare a Speech*	☐ *Make an Acrostic*
Choose at least one of your vocabulary words and design a greeting card for a person of your choice using the sentiment of that word.	Prepare a speech that includes all of your vocabulary words. Be creative in selecting the topic of the speech and how you include the words.	Make an acrostic for at least four of your weekly words. The words you choose for each letter should be related to the word written downward.
☐ *Create a Class Game*	☐ **Free Choice: Vocabulary Skills** (Fill out your proposal form before beginning the free choice!)	☐ *Design Trading Cards*
Design a class game that allows your classmates to practice their knowledge of the vocabulary words.		Create a set of trading cards for your vocabulary words. Be sure to include a meaningful sentence using each word.
☐ *Create a Crossword Puzzle*	☐ *Design a Quiz Board*	☐ *Determine Gestures*
Using all of your vocabulary words, create a crossword puzzle. Be creative in the clues that you use. Do not always use the definition for the clue!	Design a quiz board to practice your vocabulary words, their definitions, and their proper use in sentences.	Develop appropriate hand motions for all of your words to help you better understand them. Then share them with your classmates.

Check the boxes you plan to complete. They should form a tic-tac-toe across or down.
All products are due by: _____.

Parts of Speech

Game Show Menu

Reading Objectives Covered Through This Menu and These Activities
- Students will give examples of various parts of speech encountered in readings.
- Students will use resources and references to build meaning.

Writing Objectives Covered Through This Menu and These Activities
- Students will write to inform, explain, describe, or narrate.
- Students will exhibit voice in their writing.
- Students will use vivid language.

Materials Needed by Students for Completion
- Coat hangers (for mobile)
- Index cards (for mobile)
- String (for mobile)
- Poster board or large white paper
- Scrapbooking materials
- Magazines (for collage)
- Materials for board games (folders, colored cards, etc.)
- Large lined index cards (for instruction card)
- Materials for bulletin board display
- DVD or VHS recorder (for news report)
- Aluminum foil (for quiz board)
- Wires (for quiz board)

Special Notes on the Use of This Menu
This menu allows students to create a bulletin board display. Some classrooms may only have one bulletin board, so the teacher can divide the board into sections, or additional classroom wall or hall space can be sectioned off for the creation of these displays. Students can plan their display based on the amount of space they are assigned.

Students also are given the opportunity to create a game for the class. The length of the game is not stated in the product guidelines, so the teacher can determine what works best. It may be good to have students start with shorter games and work up to longer games with a review focus.

This menu allows students the opportunity to create a news report. Although students enjoy producing their own videos, there often are difficulties obtaining the equipment and scheduling the use of the video recorder. This can be modified by allowing students to act out the news report (like a play) or, if students have the technology, they may wish to produce a Webcam or Flash version of their news report.

Time Frame

- 2–3 weeks—Students are given the menu as the unit is started and the guidelines and point expectations on the back of the menu are discussed. As lessons are taught throughout the unit, students and the teacher can refer back to the options associated with that topic. The teacher will go over all of the options for the topic being covered and have students place checkmarks in the boxes next to the activities they are most interested in completing. As teaching continues throughout the 2–3 weeks, activities are discussed, chosen, and submitted for grading.
- 1 week—At the beginning of the unit, the teacher chooses an activity from each area that he or she feels would be most valuable for students. Stations can be set up in the classroom. These activities are available for student choice throughout the week as regular instruction takes place.
- 1–2 days—The teacher chooses an activity from an objective to use with the entire class during that lesson time.

Suggested Forms

- All-purpose rubric
- Oral presentation rubric
- Oral presentation feedback form
- Free-choice proposal form for point-based products

Guidelines for the Parts of Speech Game Show Menu

- You must choose at least one activity from each topic area.

- You may not do more than two activities in any one topic area for credit. (You are, of course, welcome to do more than two for your own investigation.)

- Grading will be ongoing, so turn in products as you complete them.

- All free-choice proposals must be turned in and approved *prior* to working on that free choice.

- You must earn 100 points for a 100%. You may earn extra credit up to _____ points.

- You must show your teacher your plan for completion by: _____.

Name:_____   Date:_____

Parts of Speech

Nouns	Adjectives	Verbs	Adverbs	Prepositions	Points for Each Level
☐ Design a flipbook for the different types of nouns. Include at least five examples of each type. (10 pts.)	☐ Make a mobile with at least 20 words that could replace the adjective "good" in the following sentence, yet not change the meaning: They were good students. (10 pts.)	☐ Create a collage of pictures that represent verbs. Label each verb on the back of the collage. (10 pts.)	☐ Make an instruction card that shows how to change adjectives into adverbs. (10 pts.)	☐ Make a preposition mind map that classifies all of the prepositions. (10 pts.)	10–15 points
☐ Choose your favorite short story. Predict which type of noun you think will occur the most frequently in your story. Determine the percentage of each noun type found in your story and create a pie graph to share your data. (20 pts.)	☐ Design a book cover for a thesaurus that only lists adjectives. (25 pts.)	☐ Create a board game that allows players to practice identifying and using the different types of verbs. (20 pts.)	☐ Design a bulletin board display to teach how to use adverbs in written works. (20 pts.)	☐ Create a quiz board that quizzes users on identifying prepositional phrases found in popular songs. (20 pts.)	20–25 points
☐ Create a children's ABC book with nouns that are meaningful to others your age. There will be 26 words in all, one for each letter in the alphabet. (30 pts.)	☐ Design your personal scrapbook with pages devoted to at least six different adjectives that describe you. (30 pts.)	☐ You have been named the director of a new game show called "Name That Verb." Create and perform your game show. (30 pts.)	☐ Rumor has it that Webster has decided to remove all adverbs from the English language. Prepare a news report about this phenomena and its possible impact on our lives. (30 pts.)	☐ Create a class game to practice recognizing and using prepositions properly. (30 pts.)	30 points
Free Choice (prior approval) (25–50 pts.)	**Free Choice** (prior approval) (25–50 pts.)	**Free Choice** (prior approval) (25–50 pts.)	**Free Choice** (prior approval) (25–50 pts.)	**Free Choice** (prior approval) (25–50 pts.)	25–50 points
Total:	Total:	Total:	Total:	Total:	**Total Grade:**

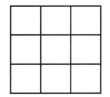

Using Reference Materials

Tic-Tac-Toe Menu

Reading Objectives Covered Through This Menu and These Activities

- Students will use resources and references to build meaning.
- Students will investigate various reference materials and their use.

Writing Objectives Covered Through This Menu and These Activities

- Students will write to express their feelings, develop ideas, reflect, or problem solve.
- Students will support their responses with textual evidence.
- Students will write to inform, explain, describe, or narrate.
- Students will write to entertain.
- Students will write to influence or persuade.
- Students will exhibit voice in their writing.
- Students will use vivid language.

Materials Needed by Students for Completion

- Poster board or large white paper
- Large lined index cards (for recipe card)
- Coat hangers (for mobile)
- Index cards (for mobile)
- String (for mobile)
- Internet access (for WebQuest)

Special Notes on the Use of This Menu

This menu allows students to create a WebQuest. There are multiple versions and templates for WebQuests available on the Internet. Teachers should decide whether to specify a certain format or allow students to create one of their own choosing.

Time Frame

- 2–3 weeks—Students are given the menu as the unit is started. As the teacher presents lessons throughout the week, he or she should refer back to the menu options associated with that content. The teacher will go over all of the options for that content and have students place checkmarks in the boxes that represent the activities they are most interested in completing. As teaching continues over the next 2–3 weeks, activities chosen and completed should make a column or row.

When students complete this pattern, they have completed one activity from each content area, learning style, or level of Bloom's, depending on the design of the menu.

- 1 week—At the start of the unit, the teacher chooses the three activities he or she feels are most valuable for the students. Stations can be set up in the classroom. These three activities are available for student choice throughout the week as regular instruction takes place.
- 1–2 days—The teacher chooses an activity from the menu to use with the entire class.

Suggested Forms

- All-purpose rubric
- Oral presentation rubric
- Oral presentation feedback form
- Free-choice proposal form

Using Reference Materials

☐ *Using a Dictionary*	☐ *Writing Resources*	☐ *Using a Thesaurus*
Create a recipe card for the proper use of a dictionary to find words. Be creative!	Write and perform a play about a debate between a dictionary and a thesaurus. Each feels that it is most useful to students your age. This debate should settle the issue!	Design a creative book cover for a thesaurus. In your editorial comments, include examples of its use and why a student should use a thesaurus.
☐ *Using a Thesaurus*	☐ ***Free Choice: Using a Dictionary***	☐ *Writing Resources*
The thesaurus is an effective resource for creating expressive language. Using the thesaurus, create a mobile with *great*, *happy*, and *big* as the top words. Under each provide at least five specific other words for each with an explanation for each word.	(Fill out your proposal form before beginning the free choice!)	Create a children's book about an abandoned dictionary and its quest to find a teenager who will appreciate it.
☐ *Writing Resources*	☐ *Using a Thesaurus*	☐ *Using a Dictionary*
Create a game show in which contestants have to use both dictionaries and thesauruses to answer the questions presented.	Using a thesaurus, write a paragraph that describes your personality and outlook on life.	Dictionaries have gone high tech! Create a WebQuest that takes questors through various dictionary Web sites, allowing them to explore and evaluate them.

Check the boxes you plan to complete. They should form a tic-tac-toe across or down.

All products are due by: _____.

Research Skills

Game Show Menu

Reading Objectives Covered Through This Menu and These Activities

- Students will compare one literary work with another.
- Students will use resources and references to build meaning.

*Writing and Research Objectives Covered
Through This Menu and These Activities*

- Students will select well-defined research questions and frame questions to direct their own research.
- Students will communicate multiple ways to organize prior knowledge about a topic.
- Students will take notes from various sources.
- Students will summarize and organize ideas gained from multiple sources.
- Students will choose the best way to present researched information.
- Students will revise drafts.
- Students will write to inform, explain, describe, or narrate.
- Students will support their responses with textual evidence.

Materials Needed by Students for Completion

- Poster board or large white paper
- Coat hangers (for mobile)
- Index cards (for mobile)
- String (for mobile)
- Microsoft PowerPoint or other slideshow software
- Materials for bulletin board display
- Large lined index cards (for instruction card)
- Cube template
- Materials for board games (folders, colored cards, etc.)

Special Notes on the Use of This Menu

This menu allows students to create a bulletin board display. Some classrooms may only have one bulletin board, so the teacher can divide the board into sections, or additional classroom wall or hall space can be sectioned off for the creation of these displays. Students can plan their display based on the amount of space they are assigned.

Time Frame

- 2–3 weeks—Students are given the menu as the unit is started and the guidelines and point expectations on the back of the menu are discussed. As lessons are taught throughout the unit, students and the teacher can refer back to the options associated with that topic. The teacher will go over all of the options for the topic being covered and have students place checkmarks in the boxes next to the activities they are most interested in completing. As teaching continues throughout the 2–3 weeks, activities are discussed, chosen, and submitted for grading.
- 1 week—At the beginning of the unit, the teacher chooses an activity from each area that he or she feels would be most valuable for students. Stations can be set up in the classroom. These activities are available for student choice throughout the week as regular instruction takes place.
- 1–2 days—The teacher chooses an activity from an objective to use with the entire class during that lesson time.

Suggested Forms

- All-purpose rubric
- Oral presentation rubric
- Oral presentation feedback form
- Student-taught lesson rubric
- Free-choice proposal form for point-based products

Guidelines for the Research Skills Game Show Menu

- You must choose at least one activity from each topic area.

- You may not do more than two activities in any one topic area for credit. (You are, of course, welcome to do more than two for your own investigation.)

- Grading will be ongoing, so turn in products as you complete them.

- All free-choice proposals must be turned in and approved *prior* to working on that free choice.

- You must earn 120 points for a 100%. You may earn extra credit up to _____ points.

- You must show your teacher your plan for completion by: _____.

Research Skills

Framing Questions	Prior Knowledge	Choosing Sources	Taking Notes	Summarizing and Presenting Information	Points for Each Level
❑ Design a poster that lists five different topics your classmates may want to investigate and at least three different questions for each topic. (10 pts.)	❑ Create a mobile that shows the different ways students may choose to organize what they already know about a topic. (10 pts.)	❑ Create an acrostic for the word *research*, writing a reliable and well-chosen source that students could use for research for each letter. (15 pts.)	❑ Create an instruction card for taking notes from online sources. (10 pts.)	❑ Make a research cube that shares six different ways you could share information you have gained through research. (15 pts.)	10–15 points
❑ Create a folded quiz book that quizzes users on their knowledge about well-written research questions. (20 pts.)	❑ Choose a topic you may want to research in the future. Create a mind map that shows how you will organize your thoughts about the topic. (20 pts.)	❑ Consider the statement: "A research paper is only as good as its sources." Design a bulletin board display centered on this statement. (25 pts.)	❑ Write a flipbook that explains how to take notes from different types of sources. Place each type on one of the flaps of the book. Include examples for each source. (25 pts.)	❑ Create a board game that allows players to go through all of the steps of the research process, from identifying a question to presenting their information. (25 pts.)	20–25 points
❑ Design a brochure that shares how to brainstorm well-written research questions, as well as how to distinguish well-written questions from those that are not. Be sure to include lots of examples! (30 pts.)	❑ Create a PowerPoint presentation that shares examples of the various ways students can organize their prior knowledge. Discuss the advantages and disadvantages of each method and rate each one for its usefulness with students your age. (30 pts.)	❑ Write and perform a play about someone who does not choose the most reliable sources before a speech. (30 pts.)	❑ Create a class lesson that teaches your classmates how to take notes from different sources. (30 pts.)	❑ Design a WebQuest that takes questors through Web sites that show different ways to present your researched information. Be sure to have questors evaluate the different options for presenting the information. (30 pts.)	30 points
Free Choice (prior approval) (25–50 pts.)	**Free Choice** (prior approval) (25–50 pts.)	**Free Choice** (prior approval) (25–50 pts.)	**Free Choice** (prior approval) (25–50 pts.)	**Free Choice** (prior approval) (25–50 pts.)	25–50 points
Total:	Total:	Total:	Total:	Total:	**Total Grade:**

Research Skills Cube

Use the cube template to show six different ways you could share information you have gained through research. Provide examples of each method and how to access that method. Use this pattern or create your own cube.

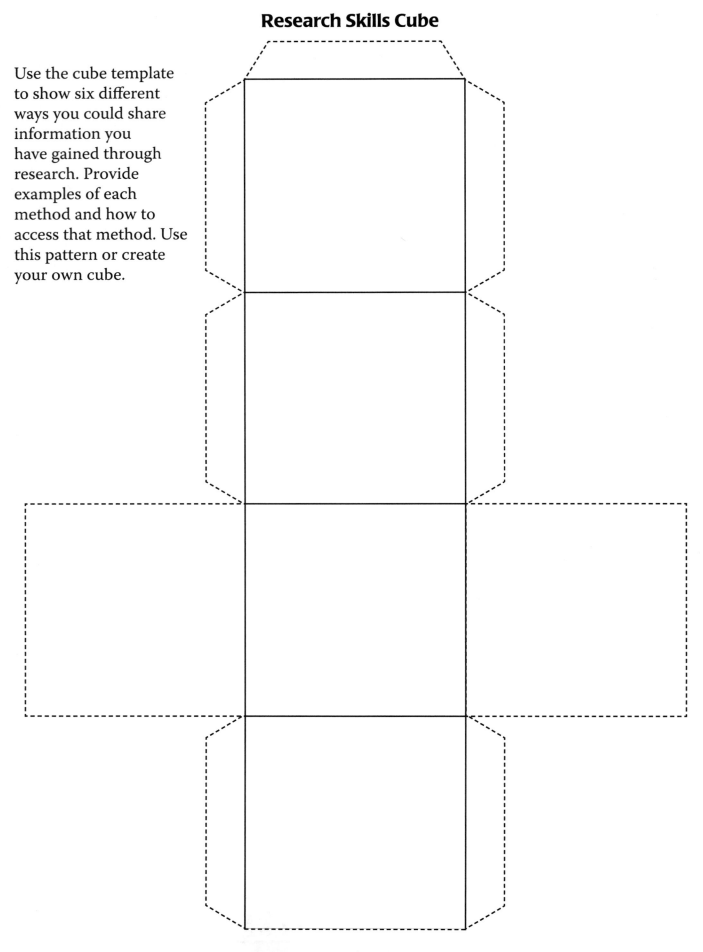

Author's Purpose

Tic-Tac-Toe Menu

Reading Objectives Covered Through This Menu and These Activities

- Students will distinguish between an author's opinion and fact.
- Students will investigate works written to persuade, inform, and entertain.
- Students will be able to identify characteristics of each type of writing.

Writing Objectives Covered Through This Menu and These Activities

- Students will write to express their feelings, develop ideas, reflect, or problem solve.
- Students will write to inform, explain, describe, or narrate.
- Students will write to entertain.
- Students will write to influence or persuade.
- Students will exhibit voice in their writing.

Materials Needed by Students for Completion

- Microsoft PowerPoint or other slideshow software
- DVD or VHS recorder (for news report)

Special Notes on the Use of This Menu

This menu allows students the opportunity to create a news report. Although students enjoy producing their own videos, there often are difficulties obtaining the equipment and scheduling the use of the video recorder. This can be modified by allowing students to act out the news report (like a play) or, if students have the technology, they may wish to produce a Webcam or Flash version of their news report.

Time Frame

- 2–3 weeks—Students are given the menu as the unit is started. As the teacher presents lessons throughout the week, he or she should refer back to the menu options associated with that content. The teacher will go over all of the options for that content and have students place checkmarks in the boxes that represent the activities they are most interested in completing. As teaching continues over the next 2–3 weeks, activities chosen and completed should make a column or row. When students complete this pattern, they have completed one activity from each content area, learning style, or level of Bloom's, depending on the design of the menu.

- 1 week—At the start of the unit, the teacher chooses the three activities he or she feels are most valuable for the students. Stations can be set up in the classroom. These three activities are available for student choice throughout the week as regular instruction takes place.
- 1–2 days—The teacher chooses an activity from the menu to use with the entire class.

Suggested Forms

- All-purpose rubric
- Oral presentation rubric
- Oral presentation feedback form
- Free-choice proposal form

Name:_____ Date:_____

Author's Purpose

☐ *Entertain*	☐ *Persuade*	☐ *Inform*
Create a PowerPoint presentation that shares various examples of books and short stories that were written specifically to entertain. Your presentation should focus on the aspects of the written work that let you know if it was written to entertain.	Choose a work written to persuade others and write and perform a play that debates the issue presented in the written work.	Select a career that interests you and interview at least two people who work in that area. Create a brochure that shares the information you obtained.
☐ *Inform*	☐ **Free Choice: Writing to Entertain** (Fill out your proposal form before beginning the free choice!)	☐ *Persuade*
Create a news report that shares important information about what is happening at your school.		Choose an issue that is impacting people your age that you feel is important. Write a persuasive newspaper article to convince others to agree with your point of view.
☐ *Persuade*	☐ *Inform*	☐ *Entertain*
Parents are lobbying the state to change the age that you can get your driver's license—to age 21! Research possible reasons behind this idea and their merit. Write and perform a persuasive speech that shares your thought on this movement.	Compose a letter to your local newspaper about your school and upcoming events for the next month. You may need to interview some people at your school to obtain enough information. Send your letter to the newspaper once it has been created.	Choose an author who writes with the purpose of entertaining his or her readers. Prepare a "You Be the Person" presentation in which you come to class as your author, discuss your written works, and how you write specifically to entertain your readers.

Check the boxes you plan to complete. They should form a tic-tac-toe across or down.
All products are due by: _____.

Identifying Bias

20-50-80 Menu

Reading Objectives Covered Through This Menu and These Activities

- Students will prove conclusions using textual evidence.
- Students will analyze informational texts for author bias (e.g., word choice and the exclusion and inclusion of particular information).
- Students will compare one literary work with another.
- Students will make and explain inferences based on the written work.
- Students will use resources and references to build meaning.

Writing Objectives Covered Through This Menu and These Activities

- Students will support their responses with textual evidence.
- Students will write to inform, explain, describe, or narrate.
- Students will write to influence or persuade.
- Students will revise drafts.

Materials Needed by Students for Completion

- Large lined index cards (for instruction card)
- Microsoft PowerPoint or other slideshow software
- DVD or VHS recorder (for news report)
- Materials for bulletin board display
- Poster board or large white paper

Special Notes on the Use of This Menu

This menu allows students to create a bulletin board display. Some classrooms may only have one bulletin board, so either the board can be divided or additional classroom wall or hall space can be sectioned off for the creation of these displays. Students can plan their display based on the amount of space they are assigned.

This menu also allows students the opportunity to create a news report. Although students enjoy producing their own videos, this can cause problems in obtaining the equipment and scheduling the use of the video recorder. This can be modified by allowing students to perform their video (like a play) or if students have the technology, they may wish to produce a webcam or flash version of their video.

Time Frame

- 1–2 weeks—Students are given the menu as the unit is started, and the teacher discusses all of the product options on the menu. As the different options are discussed, students will choose products that add to a total of 100 points. As the lessons progress through the week(s), the teacher and students refer back to the menu options associated with the content being taught.
- 1–2 days—The teacher chooses an activity or product from the menu to use with the entire class.

Suggested Forms

- All-purpose rubric
- Oral presentation rubric
- Oral presentation feedback form
- Student-taught lesson rubric
- Free-choice proposal form for point-based projects

Identifying Bias

Directions: Choose two activities from the menu below. The activities must total 100 points. Place a checkmark next to each box to show which activities you will complete. All activities must be completed by _____.

---

20 Points

❑ Design an instruction card that details how to write without bias.

❑ Create a folded quiz book that has users determining examples of bias in both writing and the media.

---

50 Points

❑ Design a brochure that explains and provides examples of bias in writing and the media. Include how to recognize it and why authors and reporters may choose to use bias.

❑ Even authors with the best of intentions have difficulty being completely unbiased in their written works. Analyze the reading selection you are working with in order to determine the author's bias. Prepare a PowerPoint presentation in which you share your knowledge of bias and quotes found in your reading selection that show your author's bias.

❑ Contact a local newspaper or television reporter and interview that person about bias in his or her job. Using his or her responses, create your own news report about how bias impacts us in our daily lives.

❑ Free choice—prepare a proposal form and submit your idea for approval.

---

80 Points

❑ Create a bulletin board display that shows the different types of bias a reader could encounter. Include quotes from a current reading selection as examples of biased and nonbiased writing.

❑ Design a lesson to help your classmates identify bias in our daily lives, the media, and the literature we read.

Resources

Biography

Adler, D. A. (2001). *B. Franklin printer.* New York: Holiday House.

Aliki. (2000). *William Shakespeare & the Globe.* New York: HarperCollins.

Alter, J. (2000). *Extraordinary explorers and adventurers.* New York: Children's Press.

Alvarez, J. (1999). *Something to declare.* New York: Plume.

Anderson, J. (2000). *Rookie: Tamika Whitmore's first year in the WNBA.* New York: Dutton.

Barrett, T. (2000). *Anna of Byzantium.* New York: Laurel-Leaf.

Berenstain, S., & Berenstain, J. (2002). *Down a sunny dirt road: An autobiography.* New York: Random House.

Bragg, R. (1998). *All over but the shoutin'.* New York: Vintage.

Brooks, T. (2004). *Sometimes the magic works: Lessons from a writing life.* New York: Del Rey.

Danneberg, J. (2002). *Women artists of the west: Five portraits in creativity and courage.* Golden, CO: Fulcrum.

Donnelly, K. (2003). *Deacon Jones.* New York: Rosen.

Flowers, P., & Dixon, A. (2003). *Alone across the Arctic: One woman's epic journey by dog team.* Portland, OR: Alaska Northwest Books.

Gantos, J. (2004). *A hole in my life.* New York: Farrar, Strauss and Giroux.

Jacobsen, R. (2001). *Rescued images: Memories of a childhood in hiding.* New York: Mikaya Press.

Macy, S. (2006). *Bull's eye: A photobiography of Annie Oakley.* Washington, DC: National Geographic Society.

Stanley, D. (2000). *Leonardo da Vinci.* New York: HarperCollins.

Zoya (with Folian, J., & Cristofari, R.). (2003). *Zoya's story: An Afghan woman's struggle for freedom.* New York: HarperCollins.

Drama

Fleischman, P. (2001). *Mind's eye.* New York: Laurel-Leaf.

Gallo, D. (Ed.). (1991). *Center stage: One-act plays for teenage readers and actors.* New York: HarperCollins.

Kehret, P. (1991). *Acting natural: Monologues, dialogs, and playlets for teens.* Colorado Springs, CO: Meriwether.

Lamb, W. (Ed.). (1987). *Ground zero club.* New York: Laurel-Leaf.

Mecca, J. T. (1997). *Real-life drama for real, live students: A collection of monologues, duet acting, scenes, & a full-length play.* Nashville, TN: Incentive.

Slaight, C., & Sharrar, J. (Eds.). (1996). *Short plays for young actors.* Newbury, VT: Smith & Kraus.

Smith, R., & Avi. (1997). *Nothing but the truth: A play.* New York: Avon.

Soto, G. (1999). *Nerdlandia.* New York: Putnam.

Graphic Novels

Argones, S. (2002). *The Groo maiden.* Milwaukie, OR: Dark Horse Comics.

Briggs, R. (2001). *Ethel and Ernest: A true story.* New York: Pantheon Books.

Eisner, W. (2006). *A contract with God.* New York: W. W. Norton. (This was the "first" graphic novel originally published in 1978.)

Eisner, W., Russell, P. C., McCrae, J., Powell, E., Muth, J. J., Chelsea, D., et al. (2002). *9-11: Artists respond, volume 1.* Milwaukie, OR: Dark Horse Comics.

Gairdino, V. (1997). *A Jew in communist Prague: Volume: Loss of innocence.* New York: NBM.

Gonick, L. (1997). *Cartoon history of the universe: Volumes 1–7.* New York: Main Street Books.

Heuet, S., & Proust, M. (2001). *Remembrance of things past: Combray.* New York: NBM.

Kiyama, H. (1999). *The four immigrants manga: A Japanese experience in San Francisco, 1904–1924* (F. L. Schodt, Trans.). Berkeley, CA: Stone Bridge Press.

Marz, R. (2002). *Sojourn: From the ashes.* Oldsmar, FL: CrossGeneration.

Miller, F., & Varley, L. (1999). *300.* Milwaukie, OR: Dark Horse Comics.

Ottaviani, J. (2003). *Dignifying science: Stories about women scientists* (2nd ed.). Ann Arbor, MI: G. T. Labs.

Tanaka, M. (1996). *Gon.* New York: DC Comics.

Toriyama, A. (2000). *Dragonball Z, vol. 1.* San Francisco: Viz Media LLC.

Waid, M., McCraw, T., & Peyer, T. (1999). *Legion of super-heroes: The beginning of tomorrow.* New York: DC Comics.

Yang, G. L. (2008). *American born Chinese.* New York: Square Fish.

Poetry

Adoff, A. (1990). *Sports pages.* New York: Trophy.

Adoff, A. (1995). *Slow dance heartbreak blues.* New York: HarperCollins

Allen, T. (Ed.). (1972). *The whispering wind: Poetry by young American Indians.* Garden City, NY: Doubleday.

Appelt, K. (2002). *Poems from homeroom: A writer's place to start.* New York: Henry Holt.

Carlson, L. M. (1995). *Cool salsa: Bilingual poems on growing up Latino in the United States.* New York: Fawcett Juniper.

Corrigan, E. (2002). *You remind me of you: A poetry memoir.* New York: Push.

Fleischman P. (2004). *Joyful noise: Poems for two voices.* New York: HarperCollins.

Glenn, M. (1999). *Who killed Mr. Chippendale? A mystery in poems.* New York: Puffin.

Gordon, R. (1995). *Pierced by a ray of sun: Poems about the times we feel alone.* New York: HarperCollins.

Hughes, L. (2007). *The dream keeper and other poems.* New York: Knopf Books for Young Readers. (Original work published 1932)

Janeczko, P. B. (1988). *The music of what happens: Poems that tell stories.* New York: Orchard Books.

Janeczko, P. B. (2000). *Stone bench in an empty park.* New York: Scholastic.

Kherdian, D. (1996). *Beat voices: An anthology of beat poetry.* New York: HarperCollins.

Nye, N. S. (2001). *What have you lost?* New York: HarperTeen.

Gilroy, T., Grace, A., McKay, J., Martin, D. A., Phillips, G. L., Roth, R., et al. (2004). *The Haiku year* (2nd ed.). Brooklyn, NY: Soft Skull Press.

Von Ziegesar, C. (Ed.). (2000). *Slam.* New York: Puffin.

Science Fiction

Adams, D. (2004). *The hitchhiker's guide to the galaxy.* New York: Harmony Books. (Original work published 1979)

Allen, R. M. (2001). *The depths of time.* New York: Bantam.

Anderson, M. T. (2004). *Feed.* Cambridge, MA: Candlewick.

Bennett, C., & Gottesfeld, J. (2002). *Anne Frank and me.* New York: Putnam.

Butler, O. E. (2003). *Parable of the talents.* New York: Seven Stories Press.

Haldeman, J. (1998). *Forever peace.* New York: Ace.

Kress, N. (2004). *Crossfire.* New York: Tor.

Lowry, L. (2009). *Messenger.* New York: Bantam.

Paulsen, G. (2002). *The white fox chronicles.* New York: Laurel Leaf.

Roberts, J. M. (2003). *Hannibal's children.* New York: Ace.

Shusterman, N. (2003). *Shattered sky.* New York: Tor.

Vande Velde, V. (2004). *Heir apparent.* New York: Harcourt.

Vizzini, N. (2005). *Be more chill.* New York: Miramax.

Weaver, W. (2003). *Memory boy.* New York: HarperTeen.

References

Anderson, L. (Ed.), Krathwohl, D. (Ed.), Airasian, P., Cruikshank, K., Mayer, R., Pintrich, P., et al. (2001). *A taxonomy for learning, teaching, and assessing: A revision of Bloom's taxonomy of educational objectives* (Complete ed.). New York: Longman.

Keen, D. (2001). *Talent in the new millennium: Report on year one of the programme.* Retrieved August 29, 2008, from http://www.aare.edu.au/01pap/kee01007.htm

About the Author

After teaching science for more than 15 years, both overseas and in the U.S., Laurie E. Westphal now works as an independent gifted education and science consultant. She enjoys developing and presenting staff development on differentiation for various districts and conferences, working with teachers to assist them in planning and developing lessons to meet the needs of their advanced students.

Laurie currently resides in Houston, TX, and has made it her goal to share her vision for real-world, product-based lessons that help all students become critical thinkers and effective problem solvers. She is the author of the *Differentiating Instruction With Menus* series as well as *Hands-On Physical Science* and *Science Dictionary for Kids*.